D1068851

LOOKING FOR HOGEYE

LOOKING FOR
HOGEYE

by Roy Reed

ASBURY PARK PUBLIC LIBRARY
ASBURY PARK, NEW JERSEY

THE UNIVERSITY OF ARKANSAS PRESS
Fayetteville   1986

To Norma

Copyright © 1986 by Roy Reed
All rights reserved
Manufactured in the United States of America
90 89 88 87   3 4 5 6

Designer: Brenda Zodrow
Typeface: Palatino
Typesetter: G&S Typesetters, Inc.
Printer: Thomson-Shore, Inc.
Binder: John H. Dekker & Sons, Inc.

"The Bloody English" and "A Letter to My Great-grandfather" (under
the title "The Evolution of the Hillbilly") first appeared in *Arkansas
Times*. Reprinted by permission.
"Camp Meeting" first appeared in *Time* magazine under the title "In
Tennessee: A Family Goes to Camp Meeting." Copyright 1982 Time Inc.
All rights reserved. Reprinted by permission from *Time*.
"Abandoning the City" and "Ozarks Winter" first appeared in the New
Orleans *Times-Picayune* Sunday magazine, *Dixie*. Reprinted with
permission of *The Times-Picayune*. Other essays first appeared in *The New
York Times*. Copyright © 1970/71/74/75/76/80/81/83/84/85 by The New
York Times Company. Reprinted by permission.

The paper used in this publication meets the minimum requirements of
the American National Standard for Permanence of Paper for Printed
Library Materials Z39.48—84. ∞

LIBRARY OF CONGRESS CATALOGING-IN-PUBLICATION DATA

Reed, Roy, 1930-
  Looking for Hogeye.
  1. Reed, Roy, 1930-   . 2. Hogeye (Ark.)—
Biography.   3. Country Life—Arkansas—Hogeye.
4. Hogeye (Ark.)—Social life and customs.   I. Title.
F419.H65R447 1986   976.7'14   85-28906
ISBN 0-938626-62-0
ISBN 0-938626-63-9 (pbk.)

Contents

Preface

The lament of our time is no longer that you can't go home again. Americans of a certain station and disposition do not even know where home is any more. These essays and articles are one man's groping and shuffling and doubling back to try to discover where his heart is.

A fellow sufferer once had occasion to describe me as "a wandering nomad of the Arab tribe of Sulzberger." I think he wrote in jest, but when I read the words I felt a twinge of familiar pain. A taste for travel is to a newspaper correspondent what a full set of fingers is to an automobile mechanic. Traveling is important, but it is not at all glamorous. And, after a few years, incessant travel tires and diminishes a man as few other exertions can. During the last of the years that I traveled for the Sulzberger family's newspaper, *The New York Times*, the fatigue became so debilitating that I longed just to go home and be still. I had no doubt where home was. It was Arkansas, where I was born. I knew with some precision where it was in Arkansas. It was not my birthplace, Hot Springs, which had been appropriated by ghosts, but a piece of Ozarks land I had bought in a hamlet called Hogeye.

I have now lived in Hogeye seven years, and I am proud to say that it is my favorite place. Whether it is home is another matter. A man who has lived in many places will probably feel a little at home in all of them. That is a pleasant feeling, but it is not a comfort in your old age.

I think my problem at Hogeye is the boots. I wear the wrong kind. The others, the men and boys who are entirely at home here, all wear cowboy boots. At work sometimes they wear the same low-heeled boots that I use around the barn lot, but they change into western boots when they dress up. That is not an affectation; these men nowadays work more cattle than the average Texan. My friend Norman Findahl, who lives down the road, grew up on a ranch in North Dakota. He has never worn anything but cowboy boots. His son Mark, whose wide open spaces have been bounded all his life by Tink Mountain and Hogeye Creek, wears cowboy boots with the same aplomb as his father. So do all the men of the community who know that they belong here.

Do I belong here? I will have no doubt of it on the Saturday morning when I can lean back in a seat at the Washington County Sale Barn, prop my feet on the bench in front of me, and be as unaware as everyone around me that my boot heels are two inches high, and that my initials are burnt into the leather uppers.

I am at least certain of this: The rural South is where I feel most nearly at home after the years of wandering. That is where most of these stories and essays are set. Many were in the nature of experiment. *The New York Times*, voice of the urban East, consciously began to look to the hinterlands during the 1950s. The first cautious glances tended to be toward the Great Issues—civil rights, economics, politics. Then a small-town North Carolinian named Gene Roberts became the national editor in 1969, and he surrounded himself with editors and correspondents who raised new questions. New, at least, for the *Times*. How do people live in the West, the Midwest, and the South? What do they worry about and celebrate? How do they think? Who *are* they? I left Washington, where I had covered the White House and other lofty problems, and moved back south to join this new effort. I felt like Bre'r Rabbit re-entering the briar patch.

Not all of these pieces were written for the *Times*. "A Letter to My Great-Grandfather" was written as a lecture for the Center for Arkansas and Regional Studies at the University of Arkansas. Both that and "The Bloody English" were first published in the *Arkansas Times* magazine. "Abandoning the City" and "Ozarks Winter" were written for the New Orleans *Times-Picayune*'s Sunday magazine, *Dixie*. "Camp Meeting" appeared in *Time* magazine. "The Country" was written for a history symposium at Tulane University and was then printed in the Tulane alumni magazine and in an anthology called *Dixie Dateline*, edited by Professor John Boles. My thanks to all for allowing the stories and essays to be used here.

And a special thanks to an old friend in Gomorrah. David R. Jones succeeded Gene Roberts as national editor of the *Times*. It was he who prodded and provoked me into writing most of these articles. On a slow day in New York, he would run me down by telephone—often flushing me at Hogeye, where I had thought to hide a while—and demand, "What's going on down there?" I always denied that anything was going on. He was never satisfied with that, and after a line of questioning that a prosecuting attorney would envy he would make me admit that the South was in the throes of the Dog Days, or vacation Bible school, or the autumn wood-cutting.

That is the way a good editor spends his days. Every writer should have one.

Roy Reed
November 21, 1985

LOOKING FOR HOGEYE

Heading Home

We left Heathrow Airport two hours late because of the fog, and were lucky at that. Behind us were travelers who had been in the terminal all night: Hindu women in saris, tending children; haggard Scots drinking whiskey. When we reached the Atlantic, the two of us drank a private toast with airline champagne. First, to England—thanks and goodbye. Then to each other, and an end to wandering. Seth and Clarrissa Timmons met us at the Fayetteville Airport. They took us to Hogeye, and we declared ourselves at home.

There have been surprises in the years since. We were barely on the ground in Arkansas when we met the first one. We had prepared for all the rigors of change that we could think of—no more international cuisine, no more week-end trips to "the continent," no more exotic intellects (a mistaken assumption), no more of the world's best theater, dominoes at the kitchen table instead of beer at the pub. What we had forgotten was the thrilling, frightening sharpness of the seasons in the Ozark Mountains.

We got to Hogeye on Christmas Eve, and for the next six weeks saw almost nothing of the plain earth. We walked on ice. We shoveled snow, more in a week than we had seen in two years in London. We watched the tree limbs sink with frozen rain, and listened to them crack like rifles

1

when they broke. The woods sounded like a battlefield for days. Sometimes an entire tree would break from the weight. We lost the southern trunk of a double-stemmed ash that we had hoped would shade the summer yard of the house we planned.

The house was to rise halfway up the western side of Webber Mountain. We knew, even then, that this was a cold and windy slope. We knew that tornadoes occasionally swept up out of the Illinois River Valley and shook the mountain. But we had not counted on the power of the January ice. Truly severe ice storms occur infrequently in the Ozarks Plateau, and when they come they are long remembered, like an utterly dry summer or a neighborhood killing. At the height of the destruction, I stood on the front porch of our temporary home and counted the .30-.30 cracks of snapping limbs at the rate of one every three seconds. Half a dozen times that day I heard the roar of aged trees going down.

We went outdoors only minutes at a time during most of our first month in the country. The temperature dropped below zero several nights. It seldom rose above freezing in the daytime. I went out to put chains on the pickup tires one morning and when I came back to the fire minutes later, the job half-finished, my fingers burned with pain and my heart pumped alarmingly. Seth had told me that he did not go outside on such days except to feed the cattle.

As the winter storm stretched into a week, then two, then three, we became aware that we had moved from a mildly annoying climate, damp and always a little too chilly, to a condition of another order. We had thrust ourselves into a season of endurance. I was reminded of Walker Percy's contention that, on the Gulf of Mexico, nothing equals a hurricane for making people come alive. Something like that happens during a winter storm in the country. You do not relax outdoors, even for a few minutes. You do not go thoughtlessly on the road; a three-mile trip to West Fork is dangerous. Every outing requires preparation. You dress as

2

carefully for a trip to the yard for firewood as you do for two hours of hunting in the woods.

But there is an interesting difference. A hurricane comes up out of the Gulf fairly rapidly, completes its destruction, and dies. Like all of life there—like the fat grass and the fast, profligate flowers—a Gulf storm is sensational. A winter storm in the mountains comes stiffly, moving as an old man moves up a rocky trail. It takes its time. It creeps into every corner of every house and barn. It freezes a spoonful of water in the palm of a rock as methodically as it does a knee-deep pool in Hogeye Creek. Then it settles in and stays. It is the staying that tests the endurance of the mountain inhabitants.

We endured that endless January. We found reservoirs of patience and creativity that we had not used before. We rationed the radio. We read only newspapers, no books, before noon. We invented chores and rewarded ourselves with good wine after dark. Neither of us is blessed with an even temper, so we took extreme care in the words we passed. I learned once more, during the long, eroding days of our homecoming, that my wife was good company.

One day toward the end of the month, I went out to empty the ashes. The air felt a little gentler. The moon was already high, an hour before sundown, and as I stood looking at it a hawk came down from the woods and flew right across it. The hawk's belly was red in the shrinking light. I flew along with it a little way, to the top of the next mountain, and then I went in to the fire feeling a small blush of confidence.

My confidence has faltered often during the intervening seasons. We built the house on the western slope, beside the one-legged ash tree, and I became a country man. I soon learned that I was a fraud. Most of my life was still attached to towns: to Fayetteville for work and play; to New York for publishing and old professional ties; to Boston and Madrid because our children were there; to New Orleans, London, Washington, Atlanta, Little Rock and a dozen

3

other cities for the bonds of old friendships and the persisting values of politics and conscience.

Some of us are cursed to spend our years yearning for our country beginnings and struggling to return to nature, only to discover that we have drifted too far and have lost our way back. No sooner had I come to acknowledge that problem, however, than I learned something even more disconcerting. The longer I stayed at Hogeye, clawing at the past, the more I was trapped. It was not so much that I was discovering nature, at last; nature was discovering *me*, drawing me centrifugally into its wildness.

Pestering my rural origins, I deliberately built a house that could be heated only by wood. Then I learned with some pain that if I wanted to stay warm in January, I had to cut wood in the summer. I took too little thought of firewood one year, acting the city man, I suppose. I cut it as I needed it and stayed barely ahead of the advancing season. When the six-weeks flu drove me indoors, my friends had to cut the wood to warm my house and comfort my wife. That frightened me. What if a winter came when I could not call on friends, or had outlived them all?

The drouth of one terrible summer still exerts its evil force. I recently cut a large maple that had struggled against the drouth's wound for four years. Each spring it had put out fewer leaves, sprinkling them judiciously across its crown the way a balding man combs his thinning hair. Then one night in the fall, during an out-of-season thunderstorm, a heedless wind tore the weakened roots from the ground and blew the old maple across the road.

Earlier in my homecoming, I would have felt reproached. But that is one of the first frailties the new countryman overcomes, the reflexive feeling that he is responsible for all that goes wrong on his farm. He makes that discovery about the same time he figures out that the farm is not really his.

Nature has given up on cities, but in the country it still disciplines its tenants. It never tires of reminding them of

4

where the real authority lies. As nature sees it, my rights are the same as the coon's. And the first discipline that a wilderness creature learns is the law of the seasons.

I was strolling on the waterfront at Santa Barbara one balmy December day several years ago. A middle-aged man in a short-sleeved Hawaiian shirt approached me for a handout. He explained, in response to my questions, that Southern California was ideal for people who did not care to work because the weather never got cold enough to make them suffer. I think of the bums of California every winter. They would learn a different discipline if they lived in the Ozarks. A squirrel in Hogeye, Arkansas, that took no thought of December would run out of nuts in November. Every crow knows that, and every possum. They don't go whining for help if they come down with the flu and run out of firewood. They just die.

I am still coming to terms with the country and with nature. I had always assumed, with breathtaking hubris, that man was superior to the other creatures. I now understand that the young man who terrorizes the highways at the wheel of a pickup truck is in the same natural category as the coon that scatters the cattle feed in my barn. They are both vandals. I also understand that nature would grieve no more for me if I died at the hands of some witless pickup vandal than it would for a mother squirrel mangled in the jaws of a coyote, or for a coon that a farmer caught in his feed barrel and blew to hell with a 12-gauge shotgun.

Snow is falling outside as I sit at the typewriter. The thermometer on the porch reads five above zero. I have been watching a piece of theater.

We have two young tomcats, one black and white and the other gray and white. Black has leapt from the snow and climbed to a branch of a tree, where he crouches. Gray is trying to dislodge him. He claws the trunk and races upward, flailing at the black fur. Black whacks him in the face

5

and he flips backward, twists in the air and lands feet-first on the snow.

I am stricken with regret. I yearn to entwine myself in nature, but the simplest feat—one that my cat performs without effort—is beyond me. So for a few minutes I stand at the window and become a child. I walk in my mind to the base of the tree and look up. I select a spot fifteen or twenty feet high (that is reasonable, considering the greater size and strength of a man) and coil my muscles. I leap. I grasp the bark fifteen feet above the ground and race upward, and when I reach the top I flip backward with elfin abandon, and spin through the air.

I feel the blood gush in my veins. I feel the rush in my brain as I race again to the top of the tree and hurl myself free. For a moment, suspended in a younger season, I am as able as a cat. I am at home.

Then I come back to the stove and warm my hands.

Abandoning the City

I get up at daylight every day and venture into the cold to greet my dog. I step to the edge of the porch and look at the thermometer, usually in amazement. I bring in kindling and firewood and build up the fire so Norma can cook breakfast in a sweater instead of a mackinaw. Then I go down the slope of Webber Mountain to the barn. In the winter, carrying feed to the cattle is easy because the mud and manure are frozen. By spring, I will sink to my ankles.

I have lived this way since I abandoned the city. Before that, I began my day by bending to the mail slot of the front door of Fig Tree House and picking up the *Guardian* and the *Times* of London, and before that by stepping onto the fragrant front porch of our house on Upperline Street in New Orleans and picking up the *Times-Picayune*. I had trained all my life to be a city person, learning tennis manners and cocktail English. When I reached New Orleans, I assumed, as the people of that city do, that I would never move again. I became as mellow as an Orleanian, and was happy. Then I fled. There was an interlude in London, but even then I was in the act of flight. I landed in the Ozarks, in my native state. A rocky hillside farm became my home.

My friends continue to ask me why. New Orleans friends seem most especially puzzled. How could a sane man leave New Orleans? I am not sure how to answer.

I am not alone, of course. Multitudes of city dwellers

7

are leaving to go back to smaller communities. I discovered that in a visit to the national census bureau several years ago, and got a front-page story out of it. For the first time in a century, other places were growing faster than the cities. The country jakes were gaining on them. (Some years after that, another reporter made the same discovery and the story was on the front page again. Newspaper people wake up in a new world every morning.)

The hordes fleeing the cities give all kinds of reasons: noise, dogs, dirty air, poisoned water, broken glass on the sidewalks. Crime, of course; although that was no urgent problem at the time I left. For middle-class whites, a barking dog two houses down the street could be more disturbing than robbery and rape in those days.

When I finally came to abandon the city, the reason went beyond all that. The real reason was tension. Not the presence of it, but the absence. A person needs a well-tuned tension. I left because I had lost touch with the city's creative tension. Toward the end of my time in New Orleans, and even London, I had to choose between alcohol and an unbecoming physical exertion to stir my blood against the prevailing lassitude. I don't have to make that choice in the country. The blood stirs itself.

That may sound paradoxical—the slumbering city and the vibrant countryside. I began to suspect it was true after I had moved to the country and found that I was drinking less alcohol. I also noticed that my body was healthier, and not from "exercise." I was puzzled. Then I realized that I was working again—working hard, with purpose—and I began to understand. The city had put me to sleep. The city was ease, the country labor. The city was a hedonistic caress, the country a puritanical jab in the ribs. There is no opportunity for ease on a farm, even a small one like mine—not for anyone brought up on duty, challenge, and self-provision.

In a harsher sense, I left the uncontrollable reality of urban misery, a misery so mindlessly out of control that it

8

had become unreal, and returned to the reality of a smaller, more manageable scale. I hesitate to suggest that man-made reality is more complex than nature's. But nature's can usually be dealt with, one day at a time. Even when it flings man's puny morality in his face. For example, I have learned again where hamburger and fried chicken come from. Butchery is no longer an abstraction.

I do not advocate that everyone move to the country and cut his own firewood and kill his own meat. Many people never feel the need, and that perhaps is enviable. Nor do I pretend that I am forever cut off from the lovely iniquities of the city. I cannot be sure that I will not some-day chuck it all and go back. As the devil said to Don Juan, "Men get tired of everything, of heaven no less than of hell."

I confess that one city pulls at me with special strength at a particular season. The city is New Orleans. The season is not gaudy Mardi Gras, but the week after. For a time, after the sudden hush of Lent, the ravenous old city is not merely at ease—it is at peace. I remember Mardi Gras as being generally cold and chastening, in spite of the revelry. The days after—in my memory—were always warm with spring and contemplation. The azaleas always bloomed at that time. The mockingbird that lived in Joe Richardson's palm tree sang for me then, and overruled the carping dog that had made my winter miserable. The stricken ginger, which had put its faith in summer and nearly lost every-thing in the February frost, began during those quiet days to rebuild, new green pushing aside old brown.

Years later, the sharp vitality of those few days still draws me. I long to be in the city for that special time. But I shall not go. I must cultivate my garden.

The Country

They called us trash. They had to have an explanation, and that was it. Theirs was God's own economic system and when it failed, blame had to be placed. The black slaves were easy to explain. Even the Yankees would tell you, in private, that niggers didn't amount to anything. But if the world's greatest civilization since Greece did not produce a decent living for the majority of the white folks, there had to be a reason. The fault was not in the civilization; it was in the folks. Some folks were trash.

Maybe they were right. We have never had what it takes to build plantations. We're a little lazy, and anxious about the wrath of God. We also dislike mosquitoes and hot weather, so have stuck close to the top of the South in the hills and mountains. From the beginning, our aspiration ran to creek bottoms instead of river deltas.

Without plantations, we produced very few governors and senators and no more sheriffs than were necessary. We spun off a few preachers and distillers, but not many others in what might be called the public service. We farmed the hills and bottoms and stayed close to home, minding our own business.

Then the twentieth century came. The South got serious about the American Way: industry, towns, getting ahead. The trash began to percolate. Some went up and some went sideways, but all of us were in motion. Now, in the ninth decade, it is clear that this has turned out to be the century of the white trash. We have percolated and drifted from one end of the country to the other. We have captured all of the towns in the South and have established outposts as far away as Bakersfield and Detroit. We've got our eye on New York.

Wherever we have moved in with enough force, we have taken charge of everything that is necessary to the community. We have become the barbers, grocers, beauticians, lawyers, cooks, postmen, nurses, junkyard operators, factory workers, plumbers, car dealers, television evangelists, mechanics. We are in business. We have even gone into politics and have not stopped at the rank of justice of the peace. The rednecked peckerwood, once considered the most retiring bird in the South, has come to town and taken over.

No matter how urban the climate we've settled in, we tend to remember who we are. That makes us easy to spot. I know an Arkansas redneck who has lived in New York for twenty-five years. He is high in the editorial councils of *The New Yorker* magazine. He spends much of his enormous salary shuttling his children to a place in the country to make sure they know how to fish.

Southerners always seem to be fishing. It is a bond to the country for those who have drifted into town. I remember a warm fall day during a political season some years ago. Uncle Rube and I are fishing a long hole of water in Irons Creek. A few bass and bream are in the bottom of the boat. A beaver has been slapping the water at the lower end of the hole. One of us looks up and sees Afton Ratliff walking across his pasture. He is not in a hurry. He walks to the creek bank and shouts to Rube across the water.

"Who's your man for President?"

"Wallace!"

"They just shot him!"

He goes back to the house. We go back to fishing.

Bond is not exactly the right word. Bond suggests that

11

millions of us, as we go about our business in the cities and towns, are tied by long pieces of rope running to Aly and Buckville and Possum Kingdom, like calves staked out to graze the long grass by the highway. That is not quite accurate. Actually, we have brought the creeks and hollers to town with us.

We are country people who now, by some historical imperative that we have not given much thought to, happen to live in town. We are slowly losing our countryness—our trashiness—and in time I reckon we will lose it all. But we have not lost it yet, and the older ones among us are as redolent of manure and catfish bait as the day we left home. We think like country people. We act like country people when we can get away with it. We are country people, for a little while longer.

How much longer depends partly on the condition of the rootstock. Not all of us have strayed to the towns. A few have stayed at home, have been there all along nourishing the stock that replenishes us all. Mother of vinegar—the few drops that contain the life of the entire line and from which a new batch of vinegar can be started any time.

Call him Tom. He is that similar to a cat: crazy, night-stirring, fired by vinegar. His people have lived on the western slope of the Ozarks for generations. The community wisdom is that he is the end of the line. As a species, they say, he is as endangered as the cougar that George Penny, aged ten, reported seeing during a recent deer hunt, or the black bear that Ancel Waterson passed on a dirt road near the top of Webber Mountain.

Tom makes the theory reasonable. He almost cut his leg off with a chain saw in a fit of carelessness. He once went to the hospital for a serious, undiagnosed illness, and when the doctors wired him with tubes and electrodes, he waited until he was alone, unplugged himself and went home. At the age of twenty-one, he mortgaged the remainder of his life to buy a farm, then lost interest in it in six months. He bought a worn old car one day, and with a case of beer and a band of friends, took it to a brushy, stump-warted clearing in the woods and drove it to death in one voluptuous night.

Then he got married—not from choice but because he had knocked the girl up. His nights became as listless as his days. He finally stirred himself once more. He announced that he had heard of a terrific job in western Oklahoma, 500 miles away, and he got into his pickup and left. The betting was that the community and his wife had seen the last of him. He came back two days later. We are waiting now to record his extinction. Will it come slowly, spinning out the useless time, or quickly, like a whippoorwill dashing itself against a window?

It is easy to portray Tom as metaphor: the last of the white trash, threatened by forces he does not understand, unable to deal with the new reality, turning inward finally to destroy himself.

I am half-persuaded that it is true. I have seen Ozarks people shouldered aside and shoved onto the more remote land by retired Yankees. I have seen Louisiana Cajuns infiltrated and changed by Texas oilmen, and gullah-talking Carolinians pushed out of the marshes by retired generals. I have seen all of the back-country Southerners from Florida crackers to Tennessee hillbillies cheapened, deceived, and changed forever by television, interstate highways, throwaway plastics, and double-knit preachers.

We have seen the real estate speculators and the corporate owners of woods and farms push the price of land so high that no one, no matter how skillful—certainly not the likes of Tom—will ever again be able to buy a farm and pay for it from its own produce.

We have seen the failure of the radical alternative, the desperate city youngsters fleeing to the hills to become self-sufficient on the land. Most leave during the first winter. Those who stay end up supporting themselves with menial

13

jobs in the towns and become self-sufficient only in home-grown marijuana.

Tom's people are threatened all across the South. They are the red men who no longer remember how to hunt.

❧

I once sat beside a hospital bed with five aging women waiting for one of them to go into surgery. One of them, by way of passing the time, said, "Do y'all remember that girl that married the Richardson boy up in the Holler?"

"Wasn't that Emmie Lou Smith?"

"No, Emmie Lee Smith married Jim McClellan. I'm talking about that girl with the crooked leg. She married that Richardson boy."

"No, she didn't. I know who you're talking about. She married Henry Blocker, and they had that boy that had to go to the penitentiary."

They moved on without me, snipping and picking to untangle the memory of who was sister to whom, who the father, who the husband. And weren't they kin to us some-how on the Melton side? They talked with a curious insistence, as if the tangle needed to be dealt with before the sick woman, who was sister to two of them and double-first cousin to the other two, went into the operating room.

I had heard the same conversation all my life, with only the names shifted from one gathering to the next. Suddenly I sat marvelling at the strength of the past. In the hills, the past is personal. The conversation of my Grandfather Meredith, whose memory ran to the 1880s, was always about family and people—our people. He might recall a spectacular crop or the tragic death of an acquaintance, but he almost never spoke of public events beyond our community. He did occasionally talk of the First World War, but only as it affected some young man of the community. One fellow, for example, had shot a toe off to avoid the draft. Another had fought in France—a fine fellow, one of the best shots with a rifle you ever saw.

14

I now live within ten miles of a famous battlefield, a place in the Ozarks where the armies of the North and the South happened to come together. The people here speak of the place as they might of a spot on the highway where two carloads of strangers collided. A few families of the nearby towns work to keep the memory alive, and the county historical association invests a lot of time and sentiment in it. But the past of the country people is invested elsewhere. Among hillbillies, the past is a family affair.

Our own family, like many others, is scattered now. It ranges from Fresno to Boston, with a large representation at Hot Springs, the town nearest its Arkansas root. Only a handful are left in the back reaches of the Ouachita Mountains where the root, creeping westward from England, Scotland, Ulster and the Carolina coast, first put down in Arkansas. On the side of my mother's people—the Merediths and Meltons—the country survivors are huddled around a community called Mount Tabor in northern Garland County. My father's people settled a few miles away in southern Yell County, at a place called Aly.

The Reeds were a large, scrappy, yellow-headed family and they scrambled out of Yell County by the dozens during the Great Depression. They went to Texas, Colorado, California, anywhere that promised work and the seductions of civilization. The women had access to the Sears and Roebuck catalogue, and the men had seen Henry Ford's astonishing machine.

Of all who left, only one Reed came back to Yell County, years later, to retire. He found a single living relic of the family when he got back. Just one man had stayed behind, out of all the Reeds who sprang there, and he did not call himself Reed.

But first, Mount Tabor: small-time farming community, much like hundreds of other hill hamlets from Arkansas to Virginia. The only public buildings are a tiny store at the top of the hill and a church and graveyard down by the creek. The church is Baptist. Several of its preachers have

15

been kin to me. Half the occupants of the graveyard are kin, too, and the same can be said of the graveyard at Aly four or five mountains away.

Everybody at Mount Tabor is white and has been since the Indians retired 150 years ago. A few black slaves were kept on the larger farms in the Ouachita River bottoms ten or fifteen miles away, and a few of their descendants lived there when I was a child. A member of our family would see one occasionally, and the event would be discussed for days.

The government dammed the Ouachita about forty years ago and flooded everybody out, black and white. Our family saw a lot of black people after that, on the streets of Hot Springs, among other cities. It was at Hot Springs that I first saw a black person. I was four years old. We were visiting Aunt Sue Meredith. One of the women took me to a front window and pointed to a man walking past. He wore shabby clothes. His face was strange in a way that did not register until later. The woman told me that he was the Sack Man. I remember the chill. The Sack Man worked for the Devil, known to me as the Booger Man, and for small children he had one role: "The Sack Man will get you if you don't behave."

Mount Tabor bustled once, not with business but with small farms. The hollows and creek bottoms were settled thickly with families and each one tilled twenty or thirty acres to grow corn, oats, and kitchen vegetables. A family usually grew a little cotton for cash. Not much cotton was left in the hills by 1940, nor many people. The Depression thinned Mount Tabor as a farmer thins corn. My Grandfather Meredith hung on until World War II, then gave up and moved to Hot Springs to work as a carpenter. All of his five children had left before him.

Those who stayed in the country, including several of my cousins at Mount Tabor, took up the slack in an interesting way. At first, the newly urbanized cousins looked down at those they had left behind. The feeling was that if they had amounted to anything, if they had had any get-up-and-go, they would have moved to town and made money. Then, after a few years, the town cousins began to notice that the country cousins were doing quite well. They had annexed the land left by the emigrants, and some had become the owners of rather large acreages.

The male cousins who had moved to town always went home several times a year to hunt. Before long, the returning hunters began to yearn for what they had left behind. Now and again one would inquire discreetly about land for sale back home. Would George Tom be interested in selling a few acres of the old family land back to one of the town cousins? The cousin thought it might be nice to have a hunting cabin on the old place. Or maybe he would run a few head of cattle and get a neighbor to look after them. Late at night, around the hunters' fire, he would ask whether they knew what he would really like to do, and they would say no, and he would say, "What I'd really like to do someday is get me a place and move back up here." The country cousins would say what a fine thing that would be, and he would talk himself into a state of contentment at the prospect.

But he never made it back. He could not whip his own inertia and his wife's reluctance. He owned a late-model car and he noticed that his cousin, for all his envied land, rattled around in a worn-out pickup. The town wife had an automatic washing machine. The country wife did the washing by hand, on a rub board.

So he went on working ten hours a day clerking in the hardware store or selling $500 burial insurance policies or struggling to scrape up enough money to buy his own grocery store. And back home at Mount Tabor his cousin added two or three head of cattle to his herd each year to take the place of the abandoned cotton and sold a little pine timber to Dierks Lumber Company and during a good year would pipe water into the house or build on a new room or buy another fifteen acres from a neighbor.

17

Thus was the mother of vinegar preserved. They are still there, minor squires overseeing a new rural community: city people retired on five acres; young town couples in house trailers commuting twenty miles to work; fishing camp and motel operators; and, scattered ever thinner, a handful of the offspring of the original stock, just enough to keep the vinegar alive.

$\approx$

The country trash are not all prospering. It is easy to find pockets of economic evil—the old miners with no coal left and too little land and scattered others who prefer to stretch the welfare check in the country rather than in some mean city street.

Drive any highway through the hills and you will see half-a-dozen littered hovels in a fifteen-mile ride. These are the Toms of this generation, the hillbilly minority who still fit the label and who are steadily dying out, year by year, making space for the more adaptable, native and outlander.

Most of the heirs of the people they called white trash are now doing well where they have clung to the land. Better than the heirs of the slaves. The black Southerners who stayed in the country are now two distinct classes: those who work for the white landowners in the Deep South, tractor drivers, now paid fairly well (men like the last sharecropper on Jimmy Carter's family plantation, who earns as much as a college teacher and owns several rental houses in Plains), and, on the other hand, the castoffs who have no work and no income except welfare and who live in semi-wildness in stinking shanties at the edges of the old farms and villages.

The surviving country white people—not the gentility of the Deep South, but the ordinary people of the foothills and the mountains—are now generally comfortable. They are public-spirited, in a narrow fashion. They support the church. One of my Meredith cousins sits on the school board of the Jessieville consolidated district, even though he and his wife have no children. They are meticulous in maintaining the old graveyards. They speak out on public issues in a selective way, shyly, uncomfortable at having their opinions and thoughts revealed.

When the United States Forest Service and one of the big timber companies began clear-cutting the woods around Mount Tabor, the Merediths swallowed their shyness and spoke their anger to newspaper reporters. The clear-cutting went on, as they knew it would, and they did not mention it again except among the family.

They do not think of it as public service, but they keep alive for a while longer some of the fading country skills. An occasional fiddler and banjo player still hold out against television. They make gardens and cut firewood. Here and there is an old-timer who remembers how to butcher a hog. In emergencies, many cattlemen are pretty good jack-leg veterinarians.

The survival of the old skills is one of the main reasons for the specialness that sets apart and gives value to the remaining country people. In my own adopted community there lives a man, now approaching old age, who spends a fair percentage of his time advising the young and the newcomers on how to live in the country—how to brace a fence post, how to castrate a calf, how to find the best place to drill a well.

At least one other surviving quality sets the native country people apart and makes them special. I used to think of it often when I worked in Washington and Atlanta and in the cities and villages of Britain and Ireland. It is a quality of community that goes deeper than a name.

Hogeye, Arkansas, is not merely a place or a newspaper dateline. It is a community in a way that is difficult to imagine among city people. The secret of the hill country community—and most other rural communities that I have known—is a profound interdependence that has nothing to do with do-goodery or sentimentalism or even religion.

Country people look after one another. They have always done so. The trash take care of their own, not out of goodness but out of necessity. There is no one else to do it. If I have to have help lifting a rock out of my pasture or starting a contrary tractor motor, I do not call for a Kelly Girl—I call for Seth Timmons or Norman Findahl. If Seth needs help overhauling a motor, he does not call for the Ford dealer—he calls Jim Winn. That is the simple dictate of economics when you live long, expensive miles from the nearest town.

The benefits go beyond economics. People especially value those they depend upon and who depend upon them in return. For that and other reasons, the active shareholders in a community—the daily participants in its ups and downs, tragedies and titillations—are drawn close to history. They feel not only the undead past every day but also the present as it treads to keep abreast of history's current.

Hogeye does not profess to be concerned with the great sweeps of the world's story. History here is more personal. I replace a weathered old plank on my barn, and the plank ties me to the day that Seth Timmons nailed it to what was then his barn. Seth pulls an onion from his garden and feels a tug from the past. This year's crop is the latest in a hardy line of multipliers that his Grandmother Timmons brought in a tow sack from Tennessee in the 1800s.

City people looking for five acres and retirement paradise are beginning to distort the history and dilute the specialness of places like Hogeye and Mount Tabor. But the specialness will be with us a while longer, as long as the rootstock and the multiplier onions survive.

The price of specialness is high. Hill politics, for example, are an extension of the rural acquisitive instinct. Not a hill farmer ever lived who did not covet his neighbor's land. Those who thrive in the country are those who know how to get and keep. They do not believe in giving their gain away in welfare money or even in elemental taxation.

They see no need for frills like food stamps. Schools and even roads are supported grudgingly.

Hill people look with suspicion on genuine higher education, anything that emphasizes the arts and sciences at the expense of football. Many of the young go away to college now, and when they occasionally acquire the rudiments of an education, they find that an unbridgeable gap has opened between them and the people back home. They usually move on, talking vaguely of greener pastures.

Among those they leave behind, the circle of perspective expands far, far slower than it might in an urban place. The mind that is suspicious of education is also suspicious of distant places, people, and ideas. In a way, an Ozarks mountaineer is as limited in his outlook as any Manhattan cab driver.

Hill people are contentious, in spite of their abiding sense of community. They love a feud. A new family moved into our community a few years ago, and the wife let it be known that she preferred reading to visiting and did not appreciate neighbors dropping in unannounced. We left her alone with satisfaction.

Every community needs someone to point a hostile finger at. At Mount Tabor, one of my cousins fell out with her brothers over an inheritance or a piece of property or something of the sort, and they feuded contentedly for fifteen years.

We are strict constructionists in the interpretation of God's will. In one community only the Baptists are considered safe from Hell and, in another, only the Presbyterians or the Pentecostals. The only major doctrine that all rural Protestants agree on is that the Roman Catholic Church is obnoxious to the Lord.

One of my earliest memories is of sermons denouncing the Catholics. I remember the fear and revulsion I felt the first time I walked past St. John's Catholic Church in Hot Springs. It was the same fear and revulsion I had felt for the

Sack Man in front of Aunt Sue's house. Years later, in the late 1970s, I encountered the same feelings among the fundamentalist Protestants of Northern Ireland, and suddenly I knew where we had learned to hate.

The hatred finally withered in one small branch of my family. My Grandmother Meredith died a slow death of cancer and she spent her last three months in St. Joseph's Hospital at Hot Springs. The hospital is run by nuns. One elderly nun looked after my grandmother, visiting her several times every day, attending her suffering and her most unpleasant—you might say repulsive—disrupted functions. The two old women came to love each other. One day near the end, the old nurse said, "You are such a good patient." My grandmother replied, "No, Sister"—the very word would have gagged her once—"you are the one who's good."

❧

One more thing has to be said about our specialness. We have a streak of plain damned meanness, and it is as much a part of our history as multiplier onions. Our ancestors posted signs at the railroad stops saying "Nigger don't let the sun set on you here." They enforced the policy with clubs and guns, because we have always loved violence. A hillbilly hunter may kill a dozen squirrels from a den tree—old, young, suckling mothers, and all. He does not need that many for food. He simply likes to shoot living creatures.

I once talked to a teen-aged boy in Stone County, Arkansas, who had been shot by his grandfather. He and several other boys had gone to the old man's yard to play a Halloween prank. The man opened the door and blazed away with buckshot. He knew that one of the boys was his own grandson.

The hills exact a kind of justice. I will tell you about a great-uncle of mine who was moderately wicked and died poor, or so he thought. Uncle Josh (the name is fictitious,

22

out of deference to certain kin who might still care) was one of the huge clan of Reeds in the rocky hills of Yell County. Like many modern farmers, Uncle Josh had an independent source of income. My own is a typewriter. His was a whiskey still. He liked women, and in illicit cohabitation with a neighbor girl he produced an unacknowledged heir. The child had his mother's name, but everybody knew he was Joshua Reed's boy. He was treated as you would expect a bastard child to be treated in Yell County, Arkansas, in the first decades of the twentieth century—like trash.

All the rest of the Reeds pulled out of Yell County during the 1930s and 1940s. They laid it to the Depression, but the reason was older than that. They left to go to Gomorrah. They had heard of the finery there—linoleum rugs and Ford cars and jobs that paid $15 a week.

In Gomorrah, they did not have to sweat in the fields until sundown. Someone else milked the cows, milled the meal, and butchered the pork. Life in the hills had been especially hard on the women. They fought back bitterly when the men, once lured to town, cast reappraising eyes toward home and talked of moving back where they belonged.

As for the men, they became a lost generation once they left the hills. They died too young, beaten to death by sidewalks and store counters, by baffled anger, by strange language and clever city ways. Of the five women who sat with me that day in St. Joseph's Hospital, four had outlived the men who came with them from the hills. They are buried, all four, in a Hot Springs cemetery called Memorial Gardens. It is tended and mowed by hired strangers.

Uncle Josh's unnamed boy never managed to escape from Yell County. While the others left, he stayed and fretted with his shame and with the sorry, worn-out land. He bought a few acres, somehow. People were selling eagerly to the timber companies and the Forest Service. Thousands of acres were taken permanently out of circulation in Yell County during the Depression. Uncle Josh's boy could not compete with the big-time buyers and the government, but he held on to what he had and added more from time to time.

About twenty years ago, he got my grandfather's forty acres, where my father and most of his ten brothers and sisters were born. He turned the house into a hay barn. He now owns every scrap of Reed land in Aly, Arkansas, and more besides. His herd of cattle is one of the largest in that part of the state. As a gesture of something, he gave my grandfather's old log house to one of my uncles to be moved, rebuilt, and preserved as a kind of memento on a suburban lot at Little Rock. Nothing he has done has made him respectable, of course. But he is accepted as a man of substance, and I suppose that is more than he hoped for.

He has one other consolation. The mother of vinegar resides in him, and he knows it. He also knows where he will be buried. They will put him under a cedar tree in the community graveyard, a few steps from his daddy.

Spring Comes to Hogeye

Spring was late in the Ozark Mountains. The first week of April had passed, and the oaks and maples were only then risking a few pale green shoots, tentative little leaves that would not constitute much of a loss if another frost stole in at night on the villainous northwest air.

Ira Solenberger was also late. Practically everybody else in Hogeye had braved the hazard of frost and had planted corn, onions, English peas and Irish potatoes. A few, emulating the bold dogwood and redbud trees, which for more than a week had been blooming bright white and purple against the dark hills, had gone so far as to put out beans, squash and even tender tomato plants.

But Mr. Solenberger, who was regarded as the best gardener in Washington County, had not plowed a furrow or planted a seed. Like the craggy maple in front of his house (itself one of the oldest things in Hogeye, a relic of the Butterfield Stage era), he found that his sap was slow to rise that spring. It had not occurred to him to blame it on his eighty-six years.

"It's that old flu," he said. "Got it back in the winter and can't get rid of it. First time I've had it since 19 and 18."

He opened the door of his heating stove and threw another chunk of wood on the fire. He closed it a little sharply and glanced out the window toward his empty garden.

Every April, the main thing going on in the rural South

is vegetable gardening. A farmer might take an hour to talk politics or help a cow give birth, but the really urgent business for him, his wife and all of the children who are old enough to keep their feet off the onion sets is getting seeds and plants in the ground to take advantage of the warming days. With a little luck, the sweet corn planted in early April will have roasting ears ("roashnears," they are called) by the middle of June.

This is a pursuit that seeks every year to outwit the awful force that pushes the shoots from the oak's branches, and that turns Seth Timmons's meadow from brown to green, and impels swallows to build nests in weathered barns.

It was the same force, that spring, that pushed Ira Solenberger out the door in a hat and coat, hunched against the biting bright air blowing up from the Illinois River, to kick the dirt and study the sky, and then retreat to the house to throw another chunk of wood on the fire.

There is still a poet up the road at Fayetteville who, in those days, drove into the hills every April to study the hills and watch for Robert Frost's signs—the gold that is nature's first evidence, "her hardest hue to hold"—and for private signs of his own that stirred his spirit.

Ira Solenberger's mind ran less to poetry than to science. He was an amateur magician, and he performed magic with plants as well as cards.

"Summer before last, I grafted some tomatoes on some poke stalks."

Why?

"Just to see if they would grow."

But when he talked of nature and growth, he used words that Frost might have used, or Thoreau.

"Plow deep. There's one acre right under another acre. I plow both of them."

"Phosphorous makes things grow roots. If you get roots, you're going to get something else."

26

"I farm with a tractor. But when it gets rowed up and a-growing, I use a roan horse."

He was now in the April sun, away from the stove. His eye scanned the three and a half acres where, just a year earlier—unencumbered by the flu—he had planted rhubarb, corn, tomatoes, squash, sweet potatoes, Irish potatoes, okra, green beans, cantaloupes, radishes, onions, cucumbers and strawberries. He had harvested a bumper crop of everything. He had eaten what he wanted and sold the rest at the farmers' market on the square at Fayetteville.

He pointed to a fallow patch and said, "That's where I had my watermelons last year." He spoke in a loud, professorial voice, as if addressing the cows at the top of the hill.

"They told me I raised the biggest watermelons in Northwest Arkansas. One of them weighed eighty-three pounds.

"I've had people ask me, 'What's your secret for raising watermelons?' I tell them, 'I ain't got no secret.'"

Then, still addressing the cows, he proceeded to tell the secret. Plow the ground deep. Watermelons need more air than water, and deep plowing lets in air.

"I plow turrible deep. Eight or ten inches." He grinned with private satisfaction and moved on to a strawberry patch.

Mr. Solenberger believed in humus. He produced it by placing mulch between the rows. I once knew a Mississippi liberal who enjoyed a minor reputation as a gardener by mulching old copies of *The New York Times*. Mr. Solenberger did not take the *Times*. He used dead crab grass.

"Make sure it's rotten," he said, jabbing the air with an open pocket knife. "If you plow under something that ain't rotten, it's a detriment to you for the first season."

Many of his neighbors planted by the moon, and still do. Mr. Solenberger did not.

"I don't pay any attention to the moon, and I'll tell you why. I've got a neighbor that plants by the moon, and I

27

asked him a question one day that he couldn't answer. I said, 'You plant a seed in dry ground, when the moon is right, and it won't come up. Then ten days later it comes a rain and that seed sprouts and comes up. But by then the sign of the moon is wrong. How do you account for that?' He couldn't answer that. I don't plant by the moon. I plant by the ground."

He was troubled, though, by another phenomenon, and he was a little reluctant to talk about it. He said the frosts seemed to come later each spring, just as the force that drove him to the plow seemed to have arrived late that year.

"The timber's awful slow a-leafing out." He cast a blue eye toward the hill across the road. "When I was a boy, we weren't bothered with frost. When spring come, it come. Our spring's almost a month later than it used to be."

I asked him what he thought the reason was. He glanced at my face to see whether I was ready to accept what he had to say. He decided to risk it.

"Well, sir, I believe the world twists a little bit. You know, everything that grows twists around to the right. Follows the sun. Even our storms that come out of the Gulf, they twist to the right. It's just nature."

Why was a man of eighty-six still involved every April with the earth's greening, as if it were his own? He passed the question off quickly. He indicated that it was merely the same motive that led him to do card tricks and tell jokes and graft tomatoes to poke weed.

"I just like to be doing things."

He returned to the question later, however, sidling up to it so as not to sound too serious. He began by confessing that spring was his favorite season. I asked him why, and he said, "Life is at a high ebb in the spring."

He leaned his chair back against the porch wall and hooked his shoe heels over the lower rung. He studied the trees on the hill across the road, and then he said, "People who are getting up in years, more of them die in the winter when the days are short, and in the hours after midnight.

28

Life is at a low ebb after midnight and in the short days. Did you know that? And the shorter the days, the lower the ebb."

Thus it was the lengthening days that sent Ira Solenberger to the garden, and he could no more resist than the hapless oak bud could resist becoming a leaf.

He was also right about the other. He thrived for one more season of the high ebb. He made one more garden. Then he died in the winter, during the short days.

Last Rites

A piano deep inside the First Free Will Baptist Church sounded the opening chords of "Onward Christian Soldiers" at 8:35 a.m., five minutes late.

Seventy-five boys and girls on the graveled parking lot outside formed a single line and began marching toward the music. The formation was sober and straight as it approached the pastor at the door, but ragged and undisciplined at the end. The larger boys hung back, snickering and making faces.

The snickering stopped once the line was inside. The strong voice of a middle-aged woman was raised in prayer.

"We hope and pray, dear God, that we can do something to help these children along the way, dear God, so that when they come to the age of accountability they will be good citizens."

Thus began another day of vacation Bible school, the single most obvious activity in Charleston, Ark., and a thousand other Southern towns during the first sunny days of June. Bible school is the last rite of spring for a few million restless young people. They have finished nine months of school, and now, before they can receive their freedom, they must perform this last, week-long duty.

In this region, a final purification of the soul is deemed necessary to prepare it for the rigors and temptations of the

30

softball field, the swimming hole, the picture show, and the long hours that will be spent lollygagging on the front porch consuming comic books and peanut butter.

The Lord gets His last chance during the first two weeks of June, then the citizens who are most vulnerable are turned loose to face sloth and inertia on their own.

One Baptist, Russell Sharp, thirteen, was asked how he intended to deal with that prospect once Bible school was over.

"I'll go fishing," he said firmly. "I'll ride horses and ride my bike. I'll ride out in the country around the strip pits [left from coal mining days], and out at the rodeo arena, up here on the hill. I may take swimming lessons."

The churches at Charleston, as elsewhere, hold off the inevitable freedom as long as they can by staggering their Bible schools. Since Bible school is ecumenical, some children are sent to one session after another, the Baptist one week, Methodist the next, Catholic the next. A few unfortunate children are still captive as late as the third week of June. These poor souls sing and pray until they are hoarse, and amass huge collections of bird feeders that they have built out of coffee cans.

Charleston, population about 1,500, is twenty-three miles east of Fort Smith. It is known for practically nothing except as the hometown of Dale Bumpers. Mr. Bumpers began his political career as a member of the Charleston School Board. Without pausing, he went on to the governor's office and the United States Senate, defeating along the way Orval E. Faubus, Winthrop Rockefeller, and J. William Fulbright.

The pastures that blanket the rolling hills come right past the Charleston city limits. They are filled with Angus and Hereford and other good breeds of cattle. Charleston, like many other towns of the Southern piedmont, has no slums. Wealth and poverty are equally rare. The last time I checked, the town had three families on welfare and about

31

the same number at the other end of the economic scale. Charlestonians are as firmly middle-of-the-road in their politics as in their accumulation of worldly goods. In a place of such pervading sameness, the few high points need to be accentuated. The seasons, for example, need to be affirmed in some way that goes beyond the change in weather. That is one reason for vacation Bible school.

Bible school is not merely for children. A large percentage of the town's mothers take part. Some teach Bible classes; some teach handicrafts; some take charge and run the show. Betty Bumpers, the senator's wife, and her sister Margaret Schaffer always worked in the Bible school when their children were young.

Russell Sharp's mother, Mrs. Forrest Sharp, was one of the leaders the day I looked in on the Bible school at the First Free Will Baptist Church. About fifteen other mothers were in the congregation with the children at the opening devotional, a kind of mini-sermon.

Mrs. Sharp was the speaker. She illustrated her devotional by placing four boxes across the front of the pulpit. They were labeled "Money," "Possessions," "Pleasure," and "Jesus Christ." She called four girls to the front. The girls took turns putting their weight on the boxes. The first three boxes, which apparently were made of paper, collapsed. The children in the audience laughed. The one labeled "Jesus Christ" bore the entire weight of the fourth girl when she stood on it with both feet.

"That is the lesson," Mrs. Sharp said. "Jesus has said that His is the only foundation that will stand when life is over." There was a titter of appreciation.

Later, in a small class of older boys, Russell Sharp took his turn reading aloud from the Bible. He began with the first verse of the 17th chapter of First Kings: "Now Elijah the Tishbite, of Tishbe in Gilead, said to Ahab, 'As the Lord the God of Israel lives. . . .'"

Somewhere beyond the window a bluejay called, and

as the call penetrated the classroom Russell's cowboy boots shuffled under the bench, replying.

A few days later, I was at my farm in Hogeye pondering the season. Spring would be gone very soon. It seemed determined to be remembered. The farmers went about their work on carpet of blinding green, their way piped by warblers. Faces wore a continuous expectancy. People talked without embarrassment of the leaves' brightness, of the hills' beauty, of an unaccountable increase in the bluebird population, of a blooming rose that had not bloomed for years past. They spoke of calves that had been born, and of some that had died.

The young cat at our place, herself barely more than a kitten, had borne her first litter. The kittens had not been found. The old-timers who had followed the ways of cats said the mother had hidden them well, as female cats are taught by nature to do. Either that or the neighborhood tomcat that had fathered them, led by another impulse of nature, had killed them. We were waiting to see. Sometimes, in the country, waiting is the only thing to do.

Camp Meeting

The wood-burning cookstoves etch a fine, drifting smoke that teases the hungry children. The cabins are unpainted, weathered to a gray dignity. The windows and doorways are unscreened and open to the breeze. From the church at the edge of the camp comes the mournful tenor of "The Sweet Bye and Bye," a hymn that thrills the memory as wood smoke thrills the nose. Except for the Chevrolets and Mercedes-Benzes resting under the oaks, we might be at a Methodist camp meeting of Andrew Jackson's time. In fact, that is precisely where we are.

The camp meeting at Tabernacle Methodist Church, near Brownsville, Tennessee, may be the last survivor of the "protracted" camp revivals that swept the rural United States during the early 1800s. The one at Tabernacle has been held every summer, in war and peace, for more than 150 years. It has survived long past the time of camp meetings, and why that is so is a mystery. Perhaps one reason is the family connection. This is not only a revival, with the worshippers coming from miles away to live for a week in uncertain comfort. It is also the annual reunion of an extraordinary family, the Taylors of Tennessee.

The kinfolks reunion and camp meeting has been the beginning and end of the Taylors' year—more so than Christmas or New Year's—for eight generations. They come from all over North America, many now called Claiborne or Thornton or one of a dozen other surnames but all descendants of the Rev. Howell Taylor. The patriarch, whose body is buried on a cedar hill behind the church, was a Virginia planter. He followed his children west in 1826 and helped them establish rich plantations and un-yielding Methodism in the bear woods of Haywood County. Western Tennessee still has entire communities that are descended from the Taylors and their slaves.

The Taylors built a church as soon as they built houses. Almost from the beginning, Tabernacle had some form of annual preaching that lasted for days, usually after harvest. Tents and brush arbors gave way to wooden cabins during the late 1800s. Electricity came with the Rural Electrifi-cation Administration in the 1930s, and air conditioning for the church and the old folks' bedrooms in the 1950s. The camp now has scores of bedrooms and thirty-three kitchens.

Craig Claiborne, the food editor of *The New York Times*, was the best-known of the Taylors the year I went to the re-union. He was one of more than three hundred attending that year. He had flown south from New York. His sister, Augusta Barnwell, had driven north from Claiborne terri-tory in the Mississippi Delta. Mr. Claiborne avoided cook-ing, but he worked the kitchens.

"How do you fry your chicken?" he asked Ora Wills, one of the several dozen black cooks at the camp, as she stood over a hot wood stove.

"Well, I cut it up and soak it in salty water," she began. The food critic, whose latest cookbook had been a collec-tion of low-salt recipes, held his tongue. "Then I take it out and shake it in a big paper bag with flour batter. And then I put it in this skillet [she hefted a pan nearly the size of a washtub] and fry it in lard."

Mr. Claiborne suspended his diet for three days. When he left, he gave the camp cooking four-star praise: "It tastes exactly like the food of my childhood in Mississippi."

The purpose of the Tabernacle meeting is the same as

35

that of all the old protracted meetings: spiritual refreshment. But for many years this one has also had a subtler aim, and the secondary purpose probably explains the meeting's survival. The Taylors—prosperous and poor, farmers and bankers, old and young—come to Tabernacle to remember who they are.

They have not left their identity to chance. The first service every year, after the greetings and opening prayers, is a "heritage walk." Some of the adults gather all the children into the church and spend half of Saturday morning telling them who their ancestors were. Then they lead them through the graveyard, pointing out the tombstones of Howell Taylor and his descendants, telling, as they walk, the family stories that have been handed down so dutifully that even the eight-year-olds know them by heart.

Sunday, the main day, is a chapter out of the Old Testament. First comes the Love Feast, when all who feel moved stand, one after another, and pour out their troubles and thank God for their blessings. Tears are shed.

Then the babies born since the last camp meeting are baptized and christened. At this reunion, the Rev. Joe Thornton, president of the Kinfolks Association, baptized five babies and a boy of about seven who had somehow been previously overlooked.

They stop for dinner—that's the noon meal—then come back to church and light candles for all who have died during the year. There were eight candles this year, throwing the cycle of birth and death into temporary imbalance.

The dead are as fully present as the newborn. Bill Thornton, who lives down the road where his late father lived, began the memorial service by confessing, "Not hardly a day goes by that I don't think, 'I wonder whether Daddy would approve of what I'm doing.'"

The preacher for the week, a high-ranking Methodist named Bob Spain, put it more bluntly.

"It's not just your life," he told them. "It's a family; it's a

36

heritage. Even if you wanted to do otherwise, you dare not because all those hands are on you."

The system works. The Taylor who came farthest this year was Dorothy Walker, thirty-three, a businesswoman who made her home at Newport Beach, Cal. She had been to camp meeting almost every August since she grew up at nearby Brownsville. She recalled being puzzled during the troubled 1960s when her fellow teenagers were asking themselves who they were.

"It never occurred to me to say, 'Who am I?' I knew who I was. I was an extension of this."

She waved her arm toward the aunts and cousins gossiping under the shade trees, the children larking among the tombstones, the couples holding hands. "My roots are here. No matter what happens to me, I know I can come back here."

The Taylors, like many of the landed gentry of the South, tend to marry close to home. Frequently they marry cousins and, following family tradition, become engaged in the graveyard during camp meeting. Joe and Becky Thornton, who are second cousins, got engaged there. Their children can trace their lineage to old Howell through five lines of Taylors. How could they forget who they are, and what is expected of them?

There is one more reason that this nineteenth-century camp meeting is still alive. The Taylor men tend to attract strong women. Edmond Taylor (who proposed by taking his sweetheart to the graveyard and asking, "How would you like to have the name Taylor on your tombstone?") seems to have attracted the strongest of the lot. Averil Crafton Taylor would have held the family together while Union soldiers looted the Tennessee plantations, as some of her predecessors did. She would have left her bed at midnight to nurse the black and white neighbors dying of yellow fever, as her kind did a hundred years ago.

Averil and Edmond, who at 81 was the oldest at the

gathering, live in the ancestral home behind the graveyard. The house is more than 150 years old. They farm about two hundred acres of the original Taylor holdings. It is they, and particularly Averil, who keep in touch with the scattered kin. Averil, the unofficial matriarch of the family, cajoled and browbeat the rest into putting together a printed family history, *The Taylors of Tabernacle*, a fascinating hodge-podge of diaries, biographical sketches and family trees. It is Averil who keeps the camp humming every August. It was she who scolded the famous food critic for being late to the first meal on opening day. "I invited him to *dinner*," she said, when he had not arrived by 12:45. "He knows the difference between dinner and supper. He's been living in New York too long."

It is the women—with and without Taylor "blood"—who have provided the spiritual resources that enable the Taylors never to doubt who they are. One of the early Taylor in-laws in Virginia left the Anglicans and joined the Methodists in defiance of her husband's threat to shoot her for it. She backed him down. Women have been the ones to instruct the children in character, responsibility and "Godly values." It is the women who have taught the children not just genealogy but respect for their elders.

Someday, Averil will take up Edmond's offer and recline under a Taylor headstone. And when her grandchildren and great-grandchildren come to frolic and hear the family stories, they will say that she, too, knew who she was.

Dog Days

Seth Timmons reports that he did not sleep well the other night because of a katydid that sang outside his window from midnight until dawn, after the others had stopped.

Not only that, he says, he has been unable to get his work done lately, for no apparent reason. He believes that he is fortunate to have got his hay in, considering the way things have been going.

He is not alone. For days, the cattle have passed the afternoons huddled motionless in the shade. The cats have lain on the steps pretending to be dead and have had to be kicked out of the way by everybody going through the door.

The cats, the cattle and Mr. Timmons are all apparently beset by the same affliction. They are in the clutches of the dog days. This is the time when evil is on the land, when dogs and snakes must be watched with special care and when all living things seem to wilt under some baleful influence.

It is the time when people, even sound and mild-tempered men like Seth Timmons, are likely to become fretful and out of kilter.

In the city, dog days have come to mean little more than an ill-defined period of heat and lassitude. They have a sharper meaning in the country, especially in the rural

39

South, where the ancient ideas that were conceived in nature linger with special strength.

The dog days are those that either precede or follow—depending on varying calculations and theories—the time when the dog star, Sirius, begins to rise with the sun. Most almanacs say they begin July 3 and end August 11.

"Noted from ancient times as the hottest and most unwholesome period of the year," says the Oxford English Dictionary, and many rural people would agree.

The coming of dog days is marked by a number of natural changes in the country. The flies increase and cattle get the pinkeye. Rain becomes scarce.

Many gardens here in the Ozarks are withering in the heat. When a light shower does fall, infrequently, its main effect is to revive the ticks and chiggers.

The urgent, lonesome call of the whippoorwill is no longer heard at night, except occasionally just before dawn and far back in the woods. The dominant night sounds have become the tuneless songs of the katydids, the tree frogs, and the crickets, messengers of ennui and discontent.

In the daytime, the bobwhites and the meadowlarks have practically fallen silent and the fields are left to the bickering crows.

Nadine Findahl, who grew up in rural Minnesota and now lives on a farm here, recalls that Minnesota children were forbidden to swim in the lakes and streams during dog days because the water was stagnant and believed to be unhealthy. That is also a common belief in the South, and one that is commonly defied by the young.

Since the dog days began, it has been so dry here that the children have had difficulty finding a swimming hole full enough to swim in.

As might be expected, the rural creatures that have the most to fear from dog days are the dogs. There is an old country theory that this is the time when dogs are most likely to get rabies.

40

"When I was a boy growing up in South Arkansas," Ernie Deane, a newspaper columnist at nearby Fayetteville, says, "we were told to leave the stray dogs alone during dog days, and as a matter of fact to beware of dogs in general, because that was the time they were supposed to go mad.

"I never heard the word 'rabies' until I was grown. A lot of dogs were killed every summer because people thought they were mad dogs. Any poor dog that had a fit during dog days was probably doomed."

The late Vance Randolph, an authority on Ozarks folklore, once reported that he had been told of mountain towns that had ordinances requiring people to confine their dogs during dog days.

The connection between the dog star and dogs is obvious enough, but how does one explain the pernicious influence that Sirius is said to exert on snakes? A widespread belief in the Ozarks and elsewhere is that snakes go blind and shed their skins during the dog days. Poisonous snakes like copperheads are especially to be watched for at this time because, being blind, they will strike at any nearby sound.

But even the nonpoisonous snakes become unaccountably belligerent during dog days, according to some sources. In his book, *Ozark Magic and Folklore,* Mr. Randolph wrote, "Uncle Israel Bonebreak, an ordinarily reliable old gentleman who lives near Pineville, Mo., tells me that he has often seen black snakes, chicken snakes, milk snakes and other harmless serpents deliberately attack human beings during the dog day period."

All things considered, it is understandable in a season such as this that a man of so serene a disposition as Seth Timmons, who has heard the katydids replace the whippoorwills in this valley every July for more than seventy years, could be kept awake by a single perverse nightsinger. It is clear to his neighbors that the gravitational pull of the dog star is working on Seth. And on them all, for that matter.

Fall

Even on a Monday, when men and boys are supposed to be back at their duty, the boom of a shotgun or the crack of a .22 rifle can be heard once or twice an hour from the vicinity of Corlskin Spring.

This is not merely truancy. The gunfire affirms that the season has changed. The official opening of the squirrel hunting season is the unofficial beginning of fall almost everywhere in the South.

The first day of squirrel hunting varies from state to state, and within a state it might vary as much as a month from one year to the next. But whatever the date, that is the real beginning of fall for millions of Southerners. The first shot from the gun each fall is anticipated with an eagerness and dread that invests only a few beginnings. It is as unnerving as a season's first kiss.

It was 1943. For the next twenty-four hours, not even the war with the Japanese would matter. There are certain expectations that every Southern boy has a right to see filled at the proper time, and such a time had arrived. The uncle's voice was lifted prayerfully, uncertainly above the rumble of the pickup truck.

> *Life's evening sun is sinking low*
> *A few more days and I must go*
> *To meet the deeds that I have done*
> *Where there will be no setting sun.*

The bottle was passed to the boy for the first time, and he took it. He felt the strange heat in his throat, and later the heat of the fire against his face in the darkness, and still later the cold dew on his hair in the wildness of the morning. He felt the tightening in his chest as he pulled the trigger in earnest for the first time, and then in his head the explosion of joy and fear as the squirrel fell at his feet.

Fall began at 7:30 this October morning. A bunch of us met in a Hogeye pasture at the edge of the woods. The sun had just set fire to the dew. The older hunters, Seth Timmons and Clifford Gilstrap, took the dog named Sport and walked east. The other two, Norman Findahl III, 16, and his brother Mark, 14, walked west. I went with the brothers.

We moved slowly. The boys were hushed and tense. Their eyes searched the top branches for the telltale rustle of leaves. Their ears strained to catch the faint grinding of teeth on hickory nut or the arrogant little cackle that hunters call a squirrel's barking.

Suddenly the boys froze, took turns aiming, firing— and missing.

We went on down that hill and up another, and halfway up they fired again and brought down the season's first game, a year-old gray squirrel.

"He's young enough to fry," Norman said. The game is always "he" until otherwise established.

This was the first mere handful of game the brothers would add to the family freezer during the fall and winter. There would be rabbit, quail, deer, all of it dressed and cleaned by the same hands that killed it.

The war wore on, and the hunting each fall became a bond that tied the boy not only to the uncle but, more importantly, to his father, and tied the two of them to the ancestral woods. They went to the same woods each year and hunted the progeny of the creatures that had been hunted by the boy's grandfather and great-grandfather.

Then the son lost his taste for it. The bond was sustained for a while by a single ritual hunt each year, an annual re-enactment of the original sacrifice. Even that became impossible in time and the bond was dissolved and the son set adrift from his own blood. A few years before the father died, the government built a dam and pushed water into the hollows of their woods and covered the remaining wildness.

Norman stopped for breath in the deepening twilight. He had been in the woods all day and had just killed his last squirrel after lunging a hundred yards up a briar-covered slope, tripping over a farmer's log pile, falling head over heels into the thicket, grabbing up his shotgun and firing just as the squirrel disappeared into a cluster of leaves.

Now he was enacting the necessary last phase of the hunt: the telling of it. The story would be told again over dinner and again on the school bus the next day and still again when he next encountered those who had been his partners in the event.

"Boy, that was a luck shot," he said. "He was climbing that tree as fast as he could climb, and I could see that it was hollow in the top. I beaded down on him and just then he went behind some leaves. I just followed him on up with my gun and pulled the trigger, and out he fell."

Everybody laughed. I asked him to try to explain what he liked about hunting. He began confidently.

"I just like being out in the woods," he said. He paused and added that he liked the challenge of finding and hitting the game. Then he stopped and thought awhile.

He resumed, haltingly, and I realized that he was groping for the exhilarating mystery that puzzles every hunter: the discovery that he can detect the presence of game by some sense that is beyond hearing, seeing or even smelling. He simply knows that he has come into its presence. He has penetrated for a moment into another world.

The boy pulled back from that chasm. His face relaxed. He picked up his gun to leave and said off-handedly, "All country boys like to hunt."

44

Arkansas Traveler

A tropical rainstorm from the Gulf of Mexico, 600 miles to the south, has been flooding my pasture in Hogeye for three days. The warm air that blew in with the rain has made everybody cranky. In November, Ozark farmers are ready for frost, not summer showers. The Gulf of Mexico is as alien as New York in this far corner of the South, half an hour from Oklahoma and an hour from Missouri. The hill people of the Ozarks are Southerners, but this low-country damp reminds us that the South, like an old Ford tractor, is held together by haywire.

The hill people do not travel much, especially farther south. I have to venture down occasionally, but I try to get home before dark. The Ozarker's attitude toward travel unnerves some visitors. The mountaineer sees traveling as a symptom of rootlessness, or worse, and he closely studies the visitor to the hills to try to find clues to the disorder. The armadillo was studied the same way when it moved in from Texas a few years ago.

For those visitors who insist on coming to the Ozarks, there is a guidebook. It has no maps, no restaurant ratings, and no puffery from the Chamber of Commerce. It is a paperback from Avon Books published by arrangement with the University of Illinois Press. The author is Vance Randolph, now dead, the foremost folklorist of the Ozarks. The book is annotated by scholars. It has a lengthy introduction and two thoroughly academic prefaces. The title is *Pissing in the Snow and Other Ozark Folktales.*

The yarns are obscene by the standards of the Moral Majority. They date to the late 1800s and the early 1900s. Mr. Randolph never found a publisher who would include them in his more sedate works. Thanks to a change in taste, the tales were published by themselves in the late 1970s, shortly before the author died. They were an instant bestseller in this region. Mr. Randolph, for the first time in his life, made some money. He complained to a friend who had smuggled a bottle of whiskey into his nursing home room that he had devoted all his life to serious scholarship and now was doomed to be remembered as a dirty old man.

The tales are a thread of intellectual history. They shed light on the mountaineer's view of man in nature. If the traveler takes the time to scrutinize the hill people—while being scrutinized—he will find the same bawdy irreverence and easygoing frankness that Mr. Randolph recorded.

Most of Mr. Randolph's numerous books, including *Pissing in the Snow,* are sold at the War Eagle Fair, which is held every fall near Hindsville. The three-day fair has drawn millions of visitors since it opened in 1954 on the banks of the War Eagle River. Those who exhibit and sell their works must meet rigid standards. There is no question as to the high standards of Mr. Randolph's books, but *Pissing* causes a little skittishness among the booksellers. One fall when I dropped in at the fair, I noticed that the display set up by Clay Anderson, the Branson, Mo., magazine publisher, prominently included all of the Randolph books except that one. I learned later that he had tucked it under the counter.

A friend told me about witnessing a sale. The customer browsed a few minutes, then asked, "Is this all of Vance Randolph's books?" Mr. Anderson replied, "No, there is one more." The customer nodded and scratched his head in a show of trying to remember the title while Mr. Anderson reached under the counter. "Yeah," the customer said, "that's the one I was looking for," and the book changed hands without the title's being spoken.

I've always thought Mr. Randolph would have appreciated that delicacy. He wrote voluminously on the mountaineers' reticence. Until very recent years, a mountain man would not utter the word "bull" in front of a woman. Even "rooster" was considered forward by some.

The War Eagle Fair has other problems with standards. It has become so successful that on the third weekend of October, every road leading to War Eagle Farm is littered with makeshift "craft fairs" selling everything from good quilts and carvings to outright junk. The most nettlesome of the competitors has set up shop just across the bridge. Ernie Deane, a writer and former president of the old Fair Association, once called the upstart business "that damned flea market across the river." The last time I visited the Fair, Kentucky Fried Chicken had a concession at the rival establishment across the bridge and was underselling the Fair's fried chicken by a dollar a plate. Every fifteen minutes, the peace of War Eagle Farm was disturbed by the WHAP WHAP WHAP of a helicopter, the latest addition from across the river. The main view offered by the enterprising pilot was of the throngs at the War Eagle Fair. Mr. Deane said he heard the noise especially close once, and when he looked up, the sapsucker was not a hundred feet above the tents.

🐸

A few miles northeast of War Eagle, at Eureka Springs, the faculties of taste and discrimination have been suspended year-round. Gerald L. K. Smith, the noted anti-Semite, moved his headquarters from California to Eureka Springs several years ago. He spent millions at the old resort constructing imitations of scenes from the "Holy Land." The project includes a thoroughly anti-Semitic Pas-

47

sion Play. There is a "Christ Only Art Gallery" featuring, on the same wall, a painting attributed to Titian and a portrayal of the Last Supper made with butterfly wings.

The capstone of the late Mr. Smith's early works is an enormous statue of Christ. It is a cube with outstretched arms. The statue occupies the highest point of land at Eureka Springs and is out of sight from only a few wooded corners in the entire town.

On the other side of Eureka, on an oak-covered slope, is a religious symbol named Thorncrown Chapel. Like Mr. Smith's Holy Land, Thorncrown is nondenominational. Unlike Mr. Smith's place, the chapel does not charge for admission.

Thorncrown was designed by E. Fay Jones, an Ozarks architect who studied with Frank Lloyd Wright. The building is glass, wood and stone—mostly glass. It huddles against the hill and humbles itself among the leaves, reaching only as high as the oaks that share the slope. But honest men have been heard to gasp as they come into sight of it. An articulate agnostic of my acquaintance was struck silent as he walked inside and looked up, and I thought I saw him bow his head.

The tour buses stop first at the Christ of the Ozarks statue and finally wind up at Thorncrown Chapel. The tourists study both with the same exclamations of muted rapture, and then they snap pictures and go home.

Extremes of quality can sometimes be found under the same roof in this part of the South. I recently visited a restaurant called Lost Bridge Lodge near Garfield, on the Missouri border. The rain had just stopped. My friends and I sat in a grand dining room on top of a mountain and watched the sun go down in glory over Beaver Lake. Then came the food. The prime rib and the broiled steaks were excellent. The jagerschnitzel was chicken-fried steak in masquerade, with gristle. Side by side on the wine list were Pouilly Fuisse and Pink Catawba.

Perhaps to make up for the fraudulent schnitzel, the restaurant throws in free entertainment. The staff are all musicians and singers. Our waitress, bringing dessert, stopped in the middle of the floor and sang, "I'm Just A Girl Who Can't Say No." The hostess sang "Turn Back, Old Man" from the arm of Norman Findahl's chair, and distracted him from his sirloin.

The Ozarks have restaurants of unqualified excellence. But there may be other problems for the patron. A few miles southwest of Garfield is a grape-growing village called Tontitown, the oldest Italian settlement in the Ozarks. One night a few years ago I was eating spaghetti and fried chicken at Mary Maestri's, the oldest restaurant in Tontitown and one of the best in Arkansas. Mrs. Maestri, who was about ninety, was sitting at the back. Her son Ed was standing at my table.

"We sure need that four-lane highway," Ed said.

"You'd feel different if they were trying to build it through your kitchen instead of my farm," I said.

He went back to the cash register and pouted, and I ate my spaghetti and sulked. Both Ed and his mother are dead now. The Chambers of Commerce are still trying to build a freeway through the Ozarks, and I am still sore about it. A new generation of Maestris is in charge of the oldest restaurant in Tontitown. Their food is still excellent; I eat there every chance I get. A quarrel is one thing, but good spaghetti is something else.

The muscadine, a cousin of the scuppernong, is a wild grape that grows in much of the South. The Carolinians make wine out of it. That is their business, but the best thing that can happen to a muscadine is to be put in a glass of jelly. Muscadine jelly is tart and deep purple. It tastes as wild as a possum, and it sticks to a biscuit. It has always been the favorite jelly in the middle latitudes of the South.

Unfortunately, the muscadine grows only sparsely in the Ozarks. It does not prosper here because the climate is too cold. Ozark hillbillies who have developed a taste for muscadine jelly usually have to go about a hundred miles south into the Ouachita Mountains and compete with the hillbillies there for the stuff. The Ouachitas (pronounced Washitaws) had a bumper crop of muscadines this fall. The roadside vendors advertise the jelly as "Muskydine," "Muskydime," "Muscadime" and "Muscdime." I recently brought home a glassful labeled "Muscdine."

The Ouachitas, and all the hills that amount to anything, run out about twenty-five miles south of Grannis, Ark. Once he is that far south, the crankiest hillbilly will go on and trespass in the low country now and then. I headed south during a cold spell one winter and went all the way to New Orleans. If a man has to have a city—and I would like to see the social scientists get serious about that question—he can do worse than New Orleans.

I am hiding at Bernie Marcus's house uptown. "Yeah," he is saying, "crime is bad in New Orleans. Like everywhere else. How you like that orange?"

We have just got home with the oranges and are sampling them. In New Orleans, a man is measured by his trophies: the age of his house (as with wine, old is better), the exclusivity of his club, the glamour of his Mardi Gras krewe. The trophy that Bernie has just come home with is the kind that will cause friends to fall out in South Louisiana—a box of navels from Plaquemines Parish. Louisiana oranges are usually available only from November to January, and then in limited quantities. This is mid-February.

The French Market had smelled like roasting coffee beans and rotten onions. Bernie, who is a lawyer, sampled a strawberry under the nose of an indignant vendor and walked away without a word. His back said "lousy," but his face said "not bad."

He stopped to speak to his friend Henry Sciambra, and studied the Sciambra Company's produce while he inquired of the Sciambra family. He stopped in front of an orange crate and looked bored. The label was hidden by a sack.

"What kinda oranges?"

Mr. Sciambra glanced sideways and said, "Louisiana."

Bernie walked away, his eye on potatoes, peppers, cauliflowers. "Watcha gettin' for 'em?"

"Ten dolluhs."

Bernie studied an onion in the light of the door. The sidewalk was clear.

"Guess I'll take 'em."

I bite into the orange again. "Not bad," I reply. New Orleans is a long way from home, but a Louisiana navel is like Tontitown spaghetti. It is worth a little trouble.

Wood Cutting

Life proceeds in Hogeye, as in the city, from one event to another. The event that has occupied the thinking people of Hogeye in recent days is the annual cutting and hauling of firewood. The task caught some people by surprise.

The laggards were lulled by the length and staying power of the summer. They foolishly speculated that firewood might not be necessary this year. But they got up and found frost on the pastures a few mornings ago, and now the chain saws are rattling from every hill.

The laborers are invisible, but anyone who is out of doors can hear the symphony of their saws. The music is a little ragged. The musicians are out of practice; the tempo drags from time to time.

A certain slackness can also be seen in the management of the wood once it reaches the house. In some yards the wood is simply piled where it was thrown from the truck. Piling wood instead of stacking it has always been the custom in the Ozarks. Northerners who have moved here in recent years look at the careless woodpiles with disapproval and envy. Some, after a few years, discover the wisdom in them.

Everybody in the hills burns wood, now that propane gas is so dear. Nearly everybody, that is. Seth Timmons drilled a water well a few years ago and hit natural gas instead. As a result, wood cutting is the only event in Hogeye that Mr. Timmons does not participate in. Sometimes he will walk up on a neighbor who is sweating and shaking over a chain saw and just stand with his hands in his overalls pockets, looking studious.

This village consists mainly of farmers of varying seriousness. It has only one store and one church, and the church is out of business. The farmers raise cattle and chickens. The latter take most of the farmers' time and provide their most dependable income. Cattle are a conceit, a fanciful enterprise that turns a profit about one year out of five. Chickens keep a roof over the head and clothes on the children. Cattle, when they are not actively draining income, occasionally earn enough unexpected profit to buy a new pickup truck or a trip to Los Angeles.

Cattle are also the glue of democracy in a place like Hogeye. Two neighbors here recently spent a long evening drinking Scotch whiskey and discussing the price of cattle, with great earnestness. A stranger would never have guessed that one, with scores of cows, was one of the largest ranchers in Hogeye and the other was the owner of seven cows and a bull.

There is a Scottish weaver named John MacGregor on the Isle of Lewis and Harris. When I last heard from him, he owned a cow and a calf, and that made him the largest rancher in Carloway. Such is the scale of illusion among the landed classes that an Arkansas farmer who owns eight head of breeding stock considers himself the social equal of the greatest cattlemen in Hogeye, Arkansas, and Carloway, Scotland.

In a somewhat older conceit, Ozarks people think of themselves as descendants of the old Calvinists, stern Scots in exile. The Presbyterian Church is vigorous in this region. Many people still attend services. Even those who do not will say, if asked, that uprightness is desirable and that firewood ought to be stacked and not just thrown down in a pile.

Drinking is also frowned upon, but people here do it.

53

When the owner of the Hogeye store applied for a license to sell beer, two part-time preachers, a Presbyterian and a Baptist, circulated a petition and kept him from getting it. They argued that the young men would get drunk and endanger their lives on the highway.

They reminded the residents of the night when young David Pickering got tanked up in town and drove his employer's new pickup truck through a barbed wire fence. The truck leaped Hogeye Creek and landed upside down in Steve Lamm's pasture. Everybody, including the unscratched but abruptly sobered driver, agreed that he had endangered his life on the highway, and he did not take a drink for three weeks.

Scottish Calvinists are not brought up to say no to a preacher, so nearly everybody signed the petition. They went on drinking beer, though, and throwing the empty cans onto the highway. The cans are a form of scorekeeping in the old contest between the preachers and the Devil. The preachers have been struggling for 150 years to purify Arkansas. The cans on the road remind them that the state is as sinful as it ever was.

The problem is pace. A lot of people here would like to get by without strong drink, but they cannot get up enough moral speed. They would also like to stack their firewood in neat rows every fall, as they do in Ohio. But it is too easy to stay warm without it, and conscience seems to require less exertion here than in Ohio. Anyway, nobody in Hogeye ever freezes to death, no matter how poorly his firewood is arranged, or how late in the season he got around to cutting it.

Wolf Hunt

Seven or eight men stood talking in the circle of firelight, drinking coffee and warming themselves against the night. Then a sound came from the woods.

"Listen," one of them said. "There's Whitey, right on the river."

The race had begun. For the rest of the night, a different language prevailed in the Fourche River bottom.

The men sat silent at the fire while the dogs—Whitey, Gunner, Happy Jack, the female known as Bud Morgan's little gyp—roamed and spoke in the distant woods. The dogs, with changes in voice and pitch, sent word as they approached the wolf, lost it, found the trail again and sped through the night in an ecstasy of closing pursuit.

In the circle of the fire, it was hard to tell whether the men favored the dogs or the wolf. Fox hunting, from which wolf hunting has evolved in this region during recent years, is frequently jovial with alcoholic conversation as the hunters sit at the fire and listen to the dogs trying to deal with the fox's antics. But the wolf is hunted soberly.

"The wolf is much smarter than a fox," said Raymond Davis, one of the older hunters, during a lull in the race. "He's got to be smart. They've tried to destroy him, and he's survived."

Wolves were almost exterminated in the Southern hill country by trappers and farmers, but they have begun to come back during the last twenty years. Farmers and ranchers who once considered the wolf a menace to livestock are changing their attitude. Many now believe the wolf to be beneficial. It feeds on small animals, including rabbits, which are a nuisance to farmers, and gophers, which undermine the western pastures with their burrows.

Cattlemen like Mr. Davis dislike having a wolf killed. When their hounds occasionally catch and kill one, the men speak of it with regret.

"I go to hear the race, to hear the hounds perform," Mr. Davis said.

The drama is in the contest of wits, the forest's most intelligent animal versus the best-bred, best-trained agents of the man. It is difficult to find dogs with the courage to hunt wolves.

"You take a cur dog," said Mr. Davis, a lean, gentle-voiced man in blue overalls. "He smells a wolf and his hair will turn around backward, and he'll go to jumping up and down stiff-legged, and he's liable to run under the floor. Some hunters are satisfied with mediocre hounds. But some of us are looking for perfection."

Mr. Davis believes that the wolf savors the contest in somewhat the same way the men and the dogs do. "There used to be an old wolf that would come up to within 150 yards of the fire. He would get up on a knoll and start howling, and the dogs would take out after him. He knew what he was doing. He was ready for a race. We called him Old Toughie. He was good wolf. I don't know what happened to him."

He said he knew of a wolf that once led a pack of dogs into the path of a speeding railroad train, and of another that led the dogs repeatedly past a rattlesnake until three of them were bitten and killed. I looked for the glint in his eyes, but he kept his gaze on the fire.

The race was off to a tentative start. Seven hounds trailed the wolf through the river bottom and the adjoining ridges and thickets. They barked intermittently for an hour

56

before they found the scent hot and fresh. Then the chase changed quickly. The hounds' voices quite suddenly inclined to a steady musical roar. A tension entered the circle at the fire.

"Old Gunner's bringing him out now," Mr. Davis said quietly. His own voice had tightened.

The men became strangely absent as they listened. Having worked to train their dogs, to hone their skills and coax them beyond their fears, the men now traveled with them in the outer dark to some place of the night where a man can only dream of going, where danger is embraced and carried on flying heels, where neither the man nor the heedless dog, acting alone, could ever enter.

The first race lasted until nearly midnight. Then the dogs lost the wolf and wandered in the woods until they struck a new trail. Another race began to build as the dogs scented and searched, weaving among the hills and fields.

Most of the men had gone home by then, drifting off one or two at a time, leaving their dogs to return on their own. Finally, only Mr. Davis and the visiting stranger were left to attend the hounds as they reported the progress of the contest.

The fire burned low. The circle of light shrank in the cold night. About three a.m., Mr. Davis made a small admission. "A lot of people think we're crazy," he said. He laughed and began to talk of getting more firewood.

But the stranger, heeding another call, drove away across the hill and left the hunter in the receding circle, his bent, lean shape inclined toward the voices of the hounds. The circle slowly became a point of light, and then it gave way to Orion's Belt hanging over the river bottom.

Killing a Steer

Farmers summon their cattle for feeding by leaning back and hollering, "Ho-oooooooo! Sook-sook-sook!" Even farm children can fetch a herd from the far side of the pasture if they learn to deliver this call with enough volume and conviction.

Last week, when it came time to kill the steer, I was suddenly mystified. How do you call an animal that you are about to send to its death?

First, there was the deception. I knew, even if the steer did not, that I was luring it to the barn for something besides a bucket of grain. I was luring it to a loading chute so I could haul it eight miles down the road to be "processed," as the butcher puts it—killed, cut up, cured, wrapped and neatly labeled for my home freezer.

The immediate problem, however, had nothing to do with my fancy urban sensibilities. My farm is like every small farm in the Ozarks. It has only one loading chute, and the chute is on the side of the farm that is farthest from wherever the chosen animal happens to be at any hour. My steer had to be driven or cajoled across a quarter of a mile of woods and open pasture. The sensible way to do that would have been to lure the animal with a bucket of feed, and a proper call.

On the other hand, I had to consider my dignity. A farmer is comfortable calling his whole herd. There is an

58

easy harmony in a "Ho-ooooooo!" addressed to twenty-five or thirty animals. You are a singer dealing with an audience. But a farmer would feel absurd singing at full throat, like Luciano Pavarotti, to a single puzzled steer walking three steps behind him.

I came late to farming, and I am still learning the fine points. I knew, however, from some old family instinct, that it would not do to walk ahead of the steer in silence. The brute would not follow a silent man, even one with a bucket of coarse-ground corn in his hand.

The real problem was a lot deeper than any of this, and I might as well come clean. The real problem was that I had not spoken to this steer for three months. When I penned him up to feed him grain and fatten him for the freezer, I had quietly vowed that I would not talk to him.

That took some effort, because a farmer habitually carries on a kind of low-grade small talk as he tends his animals. At the very least, he allows himself a little light profanity or a "Get out of that hay, you hussy!" But I was determined to treat this steer impersonally. It is easy to become attached to farm animals, and I wanted to avoid that. My father-in-law, who also blossomed late in agriculture, once fattened a calf for slaughter and made the mistake of giving it a name. He could not eat a bite of the meat.

I was faithful to my scheme. Every day for ninety days, I carried grain and filled the old bathtub that was his water trough. Every day, after his initial anxiety fell away, he trotted to the feed box when he saw me coming. He developed an unsettling habit. Often, I had to set the bucket down and square the feed box or set it upright, and during those delays he would toss his head and jump a couple of inches off the ground, first with his front feet, then with his rear. If I had not taken a vow of sullenness, I would have interpreted the display as a dance of anticipation.

Now the fattening was accomplished, and it was time to take him to the barn and load him. I knew that I had to talk to get him there. I had no idea what to say, or how.

I opened the barbed-wire gate of his pen and started walking across the pasture with my bucket of corn. He stopped at the gate. He bent and sniffed the wire, suspicious. Then he stepped across it into the open field. It took a full minute for him to understand that he was free, and when he did he tossed his head and jumped. He headed away from me and ran toward the woods. Just as my hopes fell, he turned and came back. But I knew that I would lose his attention again if I did not call to him.

I was saved by one of those lucky accidents that occur mainly on poorly run farms. One of my old cows had recently had a new calf. On a properly run farm, she and the calf would have been stabled and pampered for a week or two. But on places like mine, pampering is out of the question. She had simply staked out a patch of woods and grass away from the herd so that she could tend the calf without being bothered.

From her little patch, she saw me leave the pen with the feed bucket. She and her calf had caught up with me by the time the loping steer had finished his romp and come back. The steer saw the old cow nose into the feed bucket, and was himself overcome with greed. He stuck his nose in and grabbed a quick mouthful. I retrieved the bucket and walked quickly away toward the barn. All three followed at my heels. I now had a herd, a group large enough to talk to. I looked over my shoulder and called, with some bluntness, "Come on, gang. Let's go!"

Now I am waiting for the meat to be brought back from the butcher's. It has to hang in his cooler for two weeks, curing, and that is just as well. I have needed a little curing, myself.

I was traveling in Tibet a few years ago, and one afternoon far back in the mountains I met a herdsman who invited me to spend an hour beside his fire. He shared some yak meat with me. At the risk of offending him, I asked how he squared the killing of the yak with his Buddhist reverence for life. He said you had to say a mantra, thanking the animal for its life, as you plunged the knife into its heart.

My father, in his early years, never thought to hire a butcher; he killed his hogs and calves with his own hands, and my mother and grandmother cut up the meat and cured it. Someone always paused before dinner and thanked God for the food.

We are lucky, those of us who no longer know how to pray or say a mantra or even call for help, that we can afford to pay someone else to kill our steers. And even luckier if we can pay someone to feed and water them, as well. That is the hard part, hauling the water and carrying all that corn.

Ozarks Winter

My window reveals a modest grove of maples, and they are
restless in the early wind of fall. They are green now, just
touched with the first blush of scarlet. In a week, the maples will be entirely aflame, and then I will thank God that
this particular grove is hidden from the highway, and that I
am. In another week, the highway will be a snake of cars,
vans, and trailers, each noxious segment led by a license
from Illinois at twenty miles an hour.

As a resident of the Ozark Mountains, my advice to the
tourist is to forget the fall foliage. The visitor might well
think of coming in the winter—early winter, before the
roads ice over and many of the tourist accommodations
close. These crisp fall mornings hold the promise of the
days to come, days when the air is as clear as silver, and
wood smoke pencils the slopes and bluffs, and the cattle
grow blankets. A bird looking over his property from a
cold, bare limb can be seen for a mile and heard from one
mountain to the next. By early December, the traveler has
the country roads to himself. He can drift at his own speed
and marvel at the frost on the north-facing pastures until
late in the morning. The best season in the mountains may
well be between short sleeves and long handles, the seven
or eight weeks when a man wears a wool jacket and the
pond wears a ring of ice at the shore.

The Ozarks begin north of the Arkansas River and are

about 3,000 feet higher than the Gulf of Mexico at their greatest elevation. A lot of lore has built up about Ozarks people; some of it is true. They are shy with strangers, for example. They are probably no shyer than New Yorkers, but they keep their mouths shut instead of barking to cover their problem.

Outsiders tend to think that the Ozarks are full of moonshine. That is not true. Almost no one makes moonshine any more, not for money, anyway. The big cash crop in the mountains now is marijuana. The typical patch is a half dozen plants growing with the tomatoes and okra in the kitchen garden. It is mostly for home use and barter— egg money, the old farm wives would call it. But a number of growers have begun to plant ambitiously. They have proper little plantations hidden in clearings in the national forests. Arkansas is now ranked no. 2 or no. 3 in the nation in the quality and dollar value of its marijuana. Some experts say that the product rivals soybeans in value and that it brings over $100 million a year to the state. The mountains provide ideal growing conditions for the plant—temperate climate, high altitude, proper soil, and a convenient isolation from the centers of federal law enforcement.

The ordinary tourist should not be anxious. A citizen walking Bourbon Street, Beacon Street or Broadway is never more than a few yards from the authorities of the Mafia, yet he is much more likely to be harmed by runaway cars or purse snatchers than by the constabulary of organized crime. In the same way, the Ozarks traveler is in far greater risk from sharp-driving pickup truckers than from marijuana planters. Like the Mafiosi, the growers are mainly interested in minding their own business. You are in peril only if you blunder into their operation, and you must be deep into the woods before you need to worry about land mines and shotguns rigged with trip wires.

In the moonshine days, a professional ethic was developed to protect the innocent hunter or stroller who happened onto a still in the woods. When you realized what

63

you had done, you assumed with almost a dead certainty that you were being watched by someone with a gun. If you yourself were carrying a gun, you propped it slowly and carefully against the nearest tree. Then, still moving slowly, you picked up bits of firewood and made a show of building up the fire under the boiler. A cup would always be hanging nearby, and you took the cup and drew a little liquor and tasted it. Then you poked the fire again, slowly picked up your gun and slowly walked away. The hidden spectator would realize that you had made yourself an accomplice in the illegal operation and could not testify against him. Unfortunately, the marijuana industry is too young to have developed a similar ethic. The best thing for the tourist to do is stay away from uncharted regions of the deep woods.

However, if you are impelled to wander in the national forests, you have here another advantage of a winter tour in the Ozarks. The crop has been harvested before frost, either by the planters or the feds, and the visitor can roam the woods without fear. There is the further advantage that the copperheads and black bears are less belligerent in the winter. Native hikers often prefer winter camping. They sleep in goose-down sleeping bags, and they don't worry about ticks, chiggers, mosquitoes or sudden noises.

The visitor to the Ozarks should come not looking for mythical hillbillies asleep in the yard, but prepared to see us as we see ourselves. To help the conscientious tourist, I have devised three short tours that can be completed in a weekend each. I have labeled them the Music Tour, the Wine Tour and the New Orleans Tour. The last is so named because it includes a mountain town that has phony streetcars, just like those in the French Quarter.

Music Tour

All the tours include more than the labels suggest. This one, for example, will take the visitor to one of the most awesome caverns in the United States. The tour begins at

64

Mountain View, the seat of Stone County in north-central Arkansas.

Mountain View is the chief center of old-fashioned mountain music in the Ozarks. Music is the town's no. 1 industry, just as it is in Nashville. But the Stone County music has not kept pace with the times. You will not find Dolly Parton or Glen Campbell there singing their latest brand-new up-to-the-minute hits, or a Grand Ole Opry that has sold out to rockabilly progress.

The musicians used to play at the Courthouse every weekend. There is now a new auditorium in the federally financed Ozark Folk Center. Some people thought the new auditorium would ruin the music. But many of the old-timers are glad to get a few dollars and some recognition for their performances.

No music written after 1940 can be played at the Folk Center. That means that on any given night, you will hear a lot of "The Eighth of January," "Soldier's Joy," and other old fiddle and banjo tunes. If you're lucky, you will see Mr. Floyd Holland, who lives down the road at Fox. Mr. Holland was past ninety when I last heard from him, and still playing the banjo. He is not only a first-rate musician but also a water witch of sound reputation.

I did not see Mr. Holland the last time I visited Mountain View; I was told I had just missed him. I first saw him many years ago when he was only seventy or eighty years old. Even then he appeared not to weigh more than a hundred pounds, so unless he has put on weight, against all the rules of hill living, he still does not fill up a pair of Tuf-Nut Overalls. He and a guitarist named Booger Walls, who has since died, used to share the stage with a banjo player named Bookmiller Shannon. Mr. Walls's guitar was a foot longer than he was, as I remember it. He played with his hat on, which is local custom, and he strummed the strings with an exaggerated figure-eight motion. Mr. Shannon was a couple of feet taller and somewhat younger than the other two, and out of deference to his elders he bent far down to

65

share the microphone. There they stood, faces sober—
because that, too, is local custom; no wayward grinning to
give away the inner passions and tinglings—and played
music so sweet and perfect that my soul would swoon, and
I would sit remembering my grandfather at the fiddle, and
nearly cry with bliss and regret.

The Folk Center is one of several places in town to hear
mountain music. Grandpa Jones and Jimmie Driftwood
("The Battle of New Orleans") both have private music
halls, and you can get dinner at Grandpa's. About every
third store downtown seems to have impromptu concerts
in the evenings or some connection with music-making.
Half a dozen guitar pickers showed up on the porch of
my hotel one summer and played until one or two in the
morning.

For many fans the best show in town is still the Hootenanny that first brought fame to the town a generation ago.
The Hootenanny features free-lance musicians who play
on the Courthouse lawn on summer weekends and in an
aluminum building nearby in the winter. The show is a
little ragged. Shy beginners are interspersed with fiddlers,
pickers and bluegrass singers so talented that they make
the audience shout with joy. It is not uncommon to see a
six-year-old girl jump onto the foot-high stage and dance a
jig to the music of a fiddler who is old enough to be, and
might well be, her grandfather.

For a far different spectacle, the tourist can drive ten
miles northwest of Mountain View to Blanchard Springs
Caverns. This may be the classiest tourist attraction in the
Ozarks. The Caverns are maintained by the U.S. Forest Service and are well worth the two or three hours required to
see them. The tours are carefully guided and the trails are
safe, even for the young and the elderly. The stalagmites,
stalactites, columns, rimstone terraces, flowstones, rock
draperies and coral ponds are so imaginatively lighted that
the visitor immediately understands when the guide says

these are "living caverns." The formations are still growing from water dripping across the limestone. Bats still drop manure on enormous thousand-year-old piles. Crickets scurry and blind salamanders crawl in the watery crevices.

An underground stream is the main roadway through the caverns. Early settlers suspected that a hole in the side of the mountain was connected somehow to a spring coming out at the base half a mile away. They dropped some cornstalks into the hole, heard them hit water, and waited for the stalks to come out at the spring. They did—twenty-four hours later. We still don't know how many miles of caverns that deep, groping river traverses. Only a portion of the caves and dark cathedrals have been explored.

Mountain View has scores of motel rooms, including some at the Folk Center. My favorite lodging is The Inn at Mountain View, an eleven-room Victorian house with a wraparound porch. The Inn is one of the handful of bed-and-breakfast establishments that have been opened recently in Arkansas. The manager of The Inn does a variation on the British custom. She cooks breakfast only when she has enough guests to eat a full pan of biscuits.

New Orleans Tour

Highway 7, an hour west of Mountain View, runs north and south through the least populated part of the Ozarks. At Jasper, the visitor can see the Buffalo National River, one of the nation's carefully preserved wilderness areas. The river flows free, in spite of repeated attempts by the Corps of Engineers to dam it. The corps was finally thwarted by Congress and Orval Faubus, whose reputation in other matters has obscured his interest in nature. The Buffalo has become probably the most popular canoeing stream in this part of America. "Floating the Buffalo" is the first great spring jaunt for university students far and wide. The winter canoeist has the best high water of the year.

Bluffs rise hundreds of feet above the foaming river.

They should be regarded from a distance. Arkansas loses more tourists trying to climb the bluffs than it does to the armed defenses of the marijuana plantations.

The river has plenty of isolated, attractive camping sites that are available in winter as well as summer. Floaters may camp on the gravel bars, but are warned to move to higher ground if the weather is threatening. A flash flood can raise the water level several feet in a short time.

The Jasper area is also inviting to winter hikers and backpackers. The Ozarks have numerous trails, all well maintained by government agencies but not at all civilized. One trail begins at Fairview Campground near Jasper and runs twenty-two miles west to Haw Creek Falls. This crosses the wildest part of the Ozarks. The hiker can walk for miles without seeing a house or a pickup. Just when he thinks the entire world has been roofed over with white oaks and sycamores, he emerges onto a limestone bluff and beholds a valley that may be twenty miles wide, shimmering in the sun.

Buying handicrafts in the Ozarks requires as much discrimination as selecting a house of worship in Eureka Springs. Many roadside shops advertise "native crafts," but much of their merchandise is mass-produced in Asia. A few years ago, I visited a shop near Jasper and saw a typical array: "Indian" moccasins, wood carvings of comic hillbillies, toilet paper printed with X-rated messages, odd hats and sloganed T-shirts. On one shelf I saw a figurine of Christ and right next to it a cedar plaque with the following inscription: "This is the bathroom—The job is not finished until the paper work is done."

By asking a few questions in the towns, the visitor can find shops that sell genuine, high quality crafts made by people who live in the area. One such shop is Pendergraft's, about seven miles south of Jasper on Highway 7. Here you will find close-stitched, well-designed quilts; pottery hand-thrown by local potters; exquisite wood carvings; and split white-oak baskets made by a third generation of basket weavers. You can also buy good paintings, some by Gene Pendergraft.

Gene and Ellen Pendergraft are from New York by way of Texas. She is the daughter of Ray Freemantle, a well-known watercolorist. She worked in fashion illustrating and advertising, and once owned the only advertising agency in Austin, Texas, that was run and staffed by women. Her husband was a mathematician. He was a research linguist and was a founding member of the Society for Mechanical Translation, now called the Association for Computational Linguistics.

"We did the early work in what is now word processing, among other things," he told me.

They lived in Texas twenty-eight years, then moved to the Ozarks. They were looking for elevation, sparse population, low taxes, scenery for painting, and—most of all—four seasons. What they got was a mountain top 2,200 feet above sea level with the Ozark National Forest a few miles south and the Buffalo River a few miles north. Why did they do it? Gene thought about it a long time and gave me several answers: Too much travel. Too many airline terminals and rental cars. Too many international conferences, and jet lag. Too much hotel food.

He paused, then said with a kind of grim finality, "I wanted to read my library."

A number of Gene Pendergraft's kind have drifted into the Ozarks. I am not talking about "retired" people, the worn-out Chicagoans who want nothing more than a rose garden and a convenient golf course. Gene's kind may be tired, but they are not used up. A lot of lingering genius has ended up, for some reason, in the little town of Eureka Springs, up the road from Jasper. Eureka is a tiny, alpine New Orleans. The food is good. The coffee is strong, if you know where to look. The houses and the music are from an earlier time. The streets are narrow and rough, as they are in the French Quarter. And the town is full of interesting people. Writers, retired publishers, artists, merchants and bankers tap their toes to the jazz and western alongside leather workers, religious nuts and plain old hippies. There is a dive in Eureka Springs that, except for the absence of muffulettas and Dixie beer, might be found on the Decatur Street waterfront.

There is even a New Orleans Hotel, complete with wrought-iron balcony and a cafe named the French Market.

Eureka, population 1,989, is believed to be the smallest town in Arkansas—maybe the smallest in the whole Bible Belt—that has open bars and liquor by the drink. Much of Arkansas is dry, but Eureka has been a resort about a hundred years and knows the value of a little discreet tolerance. The liquor policy has encouraged the growth of good restaurants. The Plaza, for example, serves an excellent veal sauteed in butter, cream and herbs—the kind of dish you would find in one of the better French restaurants of New Orleans. It has a wine list that included, the last time I was there, a Chateau Lafite-Rothschild 1974 and a Clos Vougeot 1976. Those may not be the best vintages of either the Bordeaux or the Burgundy, but twenty-five years ago in most parts of the Ozarks you would have had to be personally acquainted with the sheriff to find a decent vintage of Mogen David.

The typical tourist at Eureka spends a day or two shopping for baskets, eating and drinking, and listening to music. The town has several country music barns and a couple of jazz bars. The typical tourist also spends at least one evening at the outdoor Passion Play. That's the centerpiece of the vast religion-for-profit enterprise founded by the late Gerald L. K. Smith, the gifted hell-raiser, anti-Semite, and one-time brainstormer for Huey P. Long. The Passion Play draws enormous audiences from all over the rigid mid-

70

section of the United States. I've been twice, and both times I fell asleep before the Jews killed God. I was with another reporter once, and he shook me awake in time to see the climax. Another time, when I was not there, the crowd got hailed on. Several were hospitalized.

A main advantage of visiting Eureka Springs in the winter is that the Passion Play is closed after October. That means that the sensible tourist, who would have no more than academic interest in the Smith businesses, does not have to dodge tour buses carrying creation scientists from Kansas. It also leaves the mind unfretted for Thorncrown Chapel, Fay Jones's little church tucked into the woods at the edge of town. Thorncrown is open year-round except for January and February when the mountain roads are frequently impassable. It is made of stone, wood and glass, and after the leaves are gone in the fall the chapel rises so naturally into the bare frames of the trees that the worshipper cannot be sure where the earth ends and the heavens begin.

Wine Tour

Altus is six miles south of Interstate 40 about forty miles east of Fort Smith. It sits on the first rise of the Ozarks overlooking the Arkansas River. Nature favors vines in that setting, and when several Swiss immigrants settled there late in the 1800s they planted vineyards almost as soon as they built a Catholic church. The wineries produced just enough for home and local use for many years. Prohibition slowed the budding industry but did not destroy it. Then in the 1930s and 1940s the Wiederkehr family expanded its operation and became relatively prosperous producing sweet, high-alcohol wines, the kind loved by winos and little old ladies who profess not to drink.

Arkansas wine was at that dubious plateau when young Alcuin Wiederkehr decided several years ago to take on California, New York and the whole of the European wine

71

industry. He studied vines and wine making in Europe and at the University of California at Davis. Now, for the last several years, he and his relatives have been turning more and more of their grapes into dry and medium dry table wines. Wiederkehr now bottles some very presentable Cabernet Sauvignon, Chardonnay and Johannisberg Riesling. They had a couple of good years of Gewürztraminer, the great white wine of Alsace, but seem to have lost their touch for it recently. Their dessert wine, di Tanta Maria, blended from three Muscat varieties, is delicious with Black Forest cherry cake and other heavy sweets. Their Verdelet Blanc, made from a French hybrid grape, is one of the best light white wines between New York and California. The winery has won dozens of medals in national and international competitions. Tourists may take short guided tours of the winery, then sample the wines at a bar in the retail shop. Most of the wines are sold also at a Swiss-style restaurant across the driveway.

There are several smaller wineries around Altus. The Post Winery, for one, has its own generation of sons who want to move into table wines. They have made an ambitious start and are turning out two or three wines that are not aimed at the sweet tooth. Some member of the Post family is always nearby and can be induced to stop and chat if the tourist is interested in grapes.

Mathew Post Sr. is the boss. Two of his seven sons, Paul and Matthew Jr. (two T's to give the young man more visibility in his large family) work full time in the winery. Several other family members work there in the summer.

"We figured it out one time," Mr. Post Sr. told me once, "and we've got right around twenty employees. But twelve of those are all in the family."

❧

I realize that up against the wine tours of the Napa Valley or the Bordelaise, mine is a little thin. I have thrown in an added attraction. Fayetteville, an hour and a half north of Altus, is the home of the University of Arkansas. It is not a typical tourist spot. The landscape is almost all interior, a kind of Ozark mountain of the mind.

The University, as a ferment of scholars, has been distilled to a few sweet drops of intellect, thanks to generations of farsighted political leaders who understand that the way to get the best out of a teacher is to deprive him of books and force him to the street to beg alms for research. The campus is architecturally uninteresting, except for a handful of structures that were built before the discovery of the office tower, the pastel panel, and the pre-faded yellow brick. A depressing proportion of the students are no more interesting than the campus. Their main concerns seem to be football and fast-buck economics.

The visitor should walk briskly across the campus hill, keeping an eye peeled for historians in running clothes, then drop into the valley of the Frisco Lines railway. The rails divide Dickson Street, a discolored old thoroughfare that sleeps until 5 o'clock. Roger's Pool Hall accepts day visitors, as do a few cafes and secondhand bookstores. But the places that make the street famous, those that serve music and beer, wake up late.

One of the fixtures of Dickson Street is George's Majestic Lounge, just west of the railroad. The rowdies used to sit in George's beer garden and throw empty bottles at the freight trains. Today's crowd is likely to consist of some quiet teachers and the entire editorial staff of the *Arkansas Traveler*, the University's student newspaper. The student reporters and editors no longer throw beer bottles at trains, but they are intellectually rowdy. To their credit, they account for about half of all the public squabbling and wrestling with issues that go on at the University of Arkansas.

Fayetteville is serious about writing. A writers' colony is difficult touring unless the tourist knows where to look. One place is a few blocks south of Dickson Street at the

73

Hays & Sanders Bookshop. Local writers can frequently be seen lurking among the shelves.

But perhaps the best way to find the ferment of Fayetteville is to hang out at the local night clubs. I was at a Dickson Street establishment one night listening to a singer named Lucinda Williams. Miss Williams is an unusually talented young woman, not only in her singing and picking but also in her writing. She writes most of the songs she sings. As I sat listening, it occurred to me that this poet-musician was one of the visible parts of a half-hidden community in Fayetteville—a community of artists and writers that most visitors would miss. I counted four well-known writers in the audience that night. One was the singer's father, the poet Miller Williams. Another was Ellen Gilchrist, who later won the American Book Award for *Victory Over Japan,* a collection of short stories. William Harrison was there celebrating the publication, that same day, of his novel *Burton and Speke.* James Whitehead, the author of the novel *Joiner* and of perhaps the best sonnets in modern American literature, was there.

A tourist, of course, does not just drop in on a poet and say, "Gimme a drink, Jim, and say me some poems." But the discreet traveler can rub elbows with some of these luminaries by hanging around Dickson Street and by spending a little time at the Hays & Sanders Bookshop. A good start would be to spend a little money there, as well. Ask Donald Hays for a copy of his own novel, *The Dixie Association.*

There are more than a dozen serious writers at Fayetteville if you count the half dozen connected with the University's prestigious creative writing program and a scattering of ill-tempered recluses who hole up in the hills and come to town only to buy gin and groceries.

Some of the latter are leftovers from the back-to-the-land movement of the 1970s. I ran into one a few years ago, a fallen-away newspaperman as I recall, who explained with these words why he had left the city and moved to the mountains: "I wanted to mind my own business, grow my own dope, and hump my own wife." That fellow will protect his garden with a shotgun even if he is growing nothing more suspicious than purple hull peas.

Steamboat Race

In a climate where the azaleas start blooming in December and the air conditioners are turned on in March, people go to some pains to take their minds off the heat. They walk on the shady side of the street. They play golf early and work indoors. They put limes and cucumbers in their gin to heighten the illusion of coolness. And they take any opportunity for diversion.

I once attended a steamboat race. It was held on a hot summer day, and it was one of the most diverting and utterly useless things I did during the years I lived at New Orleans. Picture thousands of legitimate citizens sitting all afternoon on a river levee, drinking beer and fanning flies, to celebrate a contest of speed between two of the slowest engine-driven vehicles in the world.

The vessels were the Delta Queen, a passenger boat that plies the Mississippi and its tributaries, and the Natchez IX, a newer and somewhat smaller boat that makes short excursions out of the port of New Orleans. This was the first steamboat race at New Orleans since 1870 when the Robert E. Lee outran the Natchez VI from New Orleans to St. Louis. My race was less dramatic than the 1870 one; it began at Audubon Park and ended at Jackson Square.

What it lacked in length it made up in promotion. After days of publicity, the two captains and their pilots were placed before the television cameras for a weighing-in cere-

76

mony. Capt. Ernest Wagner of the Delta Queen noted that his boat weighed 1,650 tons while the Natchez, with the same horsepower, weighed only 1,385 tons. In spite of the opponent's advantage, he said, he would bring back the trophy—by steamboat tradition, a pair of antlers.

"I got the frame all set up for those antlers," he said.

Capt. Clarke Hawley, his rival, snorted and the Natchez pilot interjected an oath to quit his job if his boat did not win by a mile. The ceremony ended with an argument over which captain was the better calliope player.

The race was conducted with Southern precision. It was two hours late in starting, for no apparent reason. That was just as well because many of the spectators were also late. But by 3:30 both boats were at the starting line and every idle college student in town was on the levee with a six-pack of beer. So were a large number of people who gave all appearances of being dressed for work.

The Natchez won by about a mile. Her time was twenty-nine minutes. Her rate of speed was a matter of conjecture because there was some uncertainty as to whether the course was five miles long or six. The spectators gathered afterward in the shade of various bars along the riverfront to discuss the event.

As with all public affairs in Louisiana, the main topic of speculation was the likelihood of skullduggery. One person swore that the Natchez had got a fifty-yard headstart. Another claimed to have seen her stop dead still in the water a mile before she reached the finish line. Elsewhere, that would have been perceived as an effort to tighten the contest for the benefit of the spectators, or at most as a taunt to its rival. In New Orleans, in spite of the presence of hundreds of passengers on each boat who would have reported such conduct, it was seen as clear evidence that the Natchez had tried to throw the race.

Wintering among the Cajuns

New Orleans has a French restaurant named Indulgence. It occupies an old cottage at the corner of Religious and Orange Streets, a relaxed—some would say dilapidated—neighborhood that fairly reflects America's most relaxed, well-worn city. As a metaphor, Indulgence is not bad for all of south Louisiana. New Orleans and the wet, subtropical Cajun country are territories of the senses.

A New Yorker went down for a visit a while back and spent days dashing everywhere to see everything before his vacation was over. His Louisiana friends finally persuaded him to stop: stop and look, stop and talk, stop and nurse a drink in a homely bayou bar. He caught on. Even Southerners change for the better when they travel to southern Louisiana. We are all Northerners when we cross the Mediterranean frontier at Moissant Airport, and then Louisiana works its voodoo and pulls us in.

I drove down from the Ozarks recently. I spent a couple of days decompressing in New Orleans, then headed west into the bayous and prairies that have been the main home of the Acadians since Le Grand Derangement of 1755. Spanish has replaced French as the second language of New Orleans because of a steady migration of Central Americans. But in the low rural parishes of the Acadian Coast and westward into the muddy verge of Texas, Cajun French is spoken widely and in some remote villages is still the dominant language. Because of the language, and because the Cajuns are a pool of distinctiveness, the visitor sometimes feels apart and fatigued. But if he stays long enough, he is restored and quieted and sucked into the humid Louisiana pace, which contests the speed of bayous.

I arrived in winter. I went about shedding the North by choosing a hotel in the French Quarter. Croissants and strong coffee were served in the courtyard, and I studied the waving fronds of the banana trees. I spent half a day at the Fair Grounds Race Track betting on horses, and studied the Gallic noses in the stands.

After two days of mellowing, I needed a puritan fix. I decided to learn something. I phoned W. Kenneth Holditch, professor of English at the University of New Orleans. He and his partner, Cynthia Ratcliffe, are the owners of Heritage Tours. For a modest fee, they guide tourists through every quatrain and corner of literary New Orleans. Even though I had once lived in the city, I found that they surprised me at every turn.

I waited for them in the Napoleon House bar, sipping beer and listening to Berlioz. Through the high open doors I could see across the street and past the high open doors of another bar and cafe, Maspero's, which once was a slave auction house. Two pretty black girls sat eating lunch.

My guides arrived and, to avoid appearing precipitate, drank a beer. Then we walked up Chartres Street to St. Peter, over to Royal and back to St. Louis. In those few blocks, with an occasional reference to houses and squares a short distance away, they pointed out the New Orleans connections of several dozen writers.

"*Scribner's* magazine found George Washington Cable here. . . . William Faulkner lived in that second-floor apartment on Pirate's Alley. The house is for sale. We hear they're asking $750,000. . . . Truman Capote was born in New Orleans. His family lived in the Monteleone Hotel. . . . Eudora Welty visits here often. One of her stories takes place in Galatoire's. . . . John Galsworthy wrote a poem about the old St. Louis Hotel. . . . Tennessee Williams had just bought the house at 1014 Dumaine and had it renovated. . . ."

I remembered that the playwright had also spent many mornings in the courtyard of my hotel, the Maison de Ville, drinking coffee and watching the sparrows in the banana trees. His body is buried in St. Louis, but I think it pleases his ghost to reside in New Orleans with the cheeky urchins and marching jazz bands and Pete Fountain's sweet clarinet.

I drove west the next day, out through the cane fields and bayous. Every watery ditch is a plantation worked by egrets and overseen by hawks. The towns are blisters on the savanna. Houma, a rich little city of live oaks and mock French houses, is two hours west of New Orleans and I stopped there for a couple of small indulgences—a restaurant, of course, and a cold, rainy, exhilarating tour of a swamp.

I went first to the Dusenberry family's restaurant, La Trouvaille, in a country house on Bayou Petit Caillou. They fed me spaghetti, homemade root beer and bread pudding. Papa played the guitar and sang. Most of the songs were light, because Papa is a cutup, but when he sang "Evangeline" ("Ay-vahn-zhay-leen"), the story of the Acadian exile, people wiped tears, and I could not help thinking that the diaspora continues: shoved out of Canada by the British, shoved from the best Louisiana land by the Anglo sugar cane planters, and now shoved back from the rich coastal marsh by the Texas oilmen, who are impatient with the oysters, muskrats and Cajuns that get in the way of the rigs.

❧

Bayou Annie Miller turns the tables on the oilmen. Mrs. Miller is a hearty country woman who used to trap muskrats and catch snakes for a living. When the oil companies dug canals for their work boats, she started a unique

80

touring service. She runs her motorboat up the oil company canals into the swamps and points out the local color—water birds, snakes, nutria, cypress knees.

"That's a blue runner," she said, pointing to a snake on the bank. "He'll stand up like a cobra and chase you. But if you get behind him and chase him, he'll run from you. You can have a lot of fun with that fellow."

I shared the boat with a Swiss family, all of us huddled into windbreakers. We were amazed when Mrs. Miller stood in the open boat and called alligators by name.

"Candy! Baby Dee! Isabel! Come on, bay-bee. Hurry up, Bell!"

The gators were shy that morning, but Mrs. Miller was not. When she heard the Swiss speaking French among themselves, she joined them. "C'est un grand he-*ron* bleu," she said in a hardy Cajun accent. "Keep your hands inside the boat, Madame, s'il vous plait."

For the more subdued nature lover, there is Avery Island. I drove there from Houma, some ninety miles northwest on Route 90, and toured the famous McIlhenny Company Tabasco plant. Near sundown, I went into the island's Jungle Gardens and Bird Sanctuary and positioned myself at the rookery.

Thousands of egrets, ibises, herons and other waterfowl arrived at twilight, ten or twenty at a time, and settled in the trees and bamboo. I stood watching until the flapping and grumbling stopped at dark. An alligator watched with me, collaborating in stealth, from the black water beneath the observation tower. Neither of us moved for a long time. Then I blinked, and went to New Iberia and had an elegant, red-peppered crawfish Yvonne at Patout's Restaurant. The gator, I imagined, was having frog legs.

On my second day out of New Orleans I drove deep into the upper reaches of Bayou Teche, the remotest and least Anglicized part of the Cajun country. The mail boxes announce Boudreaux, Le Blanc, Theriot, Broussard. The towns are called Breaux Bridge, Arnaudville, Grand Coteau. You pass an occasional symbol of the "Texiens," an oil well pump flailing a sugar cane field to suck a different sweetness.

On the western bank of Bayou Teche sits the little town of St. Martinville, the spiritual capital of French-speaking Louisiana. More than 79 per cent of the residents of St. Martin Parish, or county, still speak the language their ancestors brought from Celtic Brittany by way of Canada.

I visited the Evangeline Oak on the bank of the bayou, where the tragic heroine waited in vain for her lover, then walked to the main street. I admired the wooden balconies and the grillwork over the old stores. As I passed St. Martin Church, a bulletin board in the yard caught my eye. The notices read:

"Good Lent—Bon Careme"

"Turn Away From Sin—Recevez Bonne Nouvelle"

"Dieu Est Amour—God Is Love"

Cajun French is more a spoken tongue than a written one. It is also used more often in the profane world than the sacred. After leaving St. Martinville I spent the evening at a restaurant and dance hall called Mulates, near Breaux Bridge. People go there to drink, eat crawfish and listen to Cajun music. The couples danced a graceful, old-fashioned two-step, and many were speaking French.

Almost all Cajuns except a few of the elderly speak English. The outsider may be confused by it. I went into a grocery in Gueydan looking for a Vermilion Parish rice that tastes and smells like popcorn. An amiable little woman of about seventy-five took me by the arm and led me to it. Then she told me, as I picked up a five-pound sack, "People roun' here don't lack it. Me, I lack rice that tastes lack rice."

The Cajuns are well known for their warmth. Strangers, no matter how presumptuous, are made welcome. For example, many of the sugar cane plantations and mills can be toured for the asking. The easy way to do this is to phone the American Sugar Cane League in New Orleans and arrange a tour. But I once wheeled into the sugar mill at Breaux Bridge on an impulse, and the manager dropped everything for an hour to show the place to me and my friends and to explain the intricacies of sugar making.

I decided on my recent trip to visit a crawfish processing plant. The dictionaries spell it "crayfish," but why should an outsider who would shrink from peeling one be allowed to spell it?

Peeling happened to be the motive of my plant visit. I had peeled several pounds for lunch the day before and my thumb was sore from shell cuts. I was out of practice. I walked into Pat's seafood packing plant at Henderson, next door to Pat's famous restaurant, and asked to watch the pros.

A woman behind the table invited me to pull up a chair and go to work. When I declined, she said with a grin, "You here to watch or learn?" I ignored her taunt and concentrated on her style. It consisted of two fast motions: off with the head, then off with the tail shell to expose the edible meat. I calculated that she could have peeled my entire lunch in ninety seconds.

When the outside world thinks of Cajun food, it thinks of crawfish, shrimp, oysters, jambalaya and gumbo. You learn of other, more primitive foods as you penetrate the Acadian Coast and the bayous. On the window of the Bienvenu Cash Grocery at St. Martinville I saw advertising for hog lard, fresh hog cracklings (cooked skins), fresh catfish, garfish, turtle and alligator meat.

One of the least known and perhaps the most addictive of the Cajun dishes is boudin. Boudin (the last syllable rhymes with can, nasally) is a sausage containing rice, pork and pork liver. Cajun children eat it like ice cream in a cone.

I have a friend in New Orleans who knows food as well as politics, law and other Louisiana weaknesses. He had told me, with some show of confidentiality, where to find the world's best boudin. It was in the town of Jennings at a cafe named the Boudin King. I found myself within fifty miles of Jennings on the next to last day of my trip, so I went. The Boudin King turns out to be not merely a cafe but also a man. Ellis Cormier, a royally built native of Jennings, started making boudin when he had a grocery store. Traditionally, the sausage is made from the scraps at "le boucherie," or hog killing.

"I started using better pork because I didn't have enough scraps," he said, "and the business grew." He claims to have created the boudin industry of Louisiana, although he admits that the claim is controversial. He uses his grandfather's recipe that originated in Nova Scotia. The seasonings include green onions, parsley, cayenne, salt and black pepper. Mr. Cormier has had customers from every state and several foreign countries. He sells 4,000 pounds a week.

I drove on to Eunice to spend the night and that evening, a Friday, I visited a bar called the Blue Goose, hoping to hear a Cajun band. But the printed schedule of bands that I had picked up in Lafayette turned out to be a rather generalized guide, like Cajun directions on the highway. The Blue Goose had a band on Sunday, not Friday.

The barmaid, whose name was Jenny, pacified me by teaching me the rudiments of bourre, the favorite card game among Cajuns. She said her widowed mother earned her living at it. The conversation turned to food, and I mentioned that I had just that day eaten the best boudin in the world.

"Ah, now, Cher," she said, "the best boudin is made here in Eunice. You go try the boudin at Johnson's Grocery."

At 7:30 the next morning I joined a fifty-foot line at the meat counter of Johnson's Grocery. All of us were buying boudin. The butcher sold me a pound wrapped in plain paper.

I drove ten miles north to Mamou, where I was to spend my last half day in the Cajun country, and carried the boudin into Fred's Lounge. I ordered a beer and began eating my breakfast—Budweiser and boudin.

Fred's Lounge was an indulgence I had promised myself. I had once spent Mardi Gras in Mamou. Some of the country Cajun towns still celebrate Mardi Gras on horse-back. Young men dress as clowns, get drunk and ride the countryside begging chickens and other ingredients for a giant gumbo. In the excitement of "courir de Mardi Gras" I had somehow missed Fred's Lounge, and had since learned that the best radio show of country Cajun music originates in Fred's every Saturday morning.

Revon Reed, the host, plays records, tells jokes and reads commercials in the old-fashioned redneck French of the Cajuns. A live band plays string music as well, and the regulars crowd the dance floor. The bar is busy by 8:30 a.m.

The barmaid filled me in on the action, a kind of running soap opera. "See that old man? That the riches' man in Evangeline Parish. He bought his wife a washing machine last year, first one she ever had in forty years, and it's a wringer machine. He comes in here every Saturday and chases the women."

Another elderly man and his woman friend came in.

"What you have, Cher?" the barmaid asked.

"Two Morgan Davids."

She returned to me and noticed what I was eating. I explained that it was the world's best boudin, from Eunice. She lifted an eyebrow and said, "Listen, Cher, the best boudin in the world is made at the grocery store right here in Mamou, down the street here." She pulled her own package of sausage from under the bar and cut a slice for me. "Now you tell *me*, Cher, isn't that the best boudin in the world?" I admitted it. She brought me another beer.

Two or three hours later I left the warm comfort of Fred's and went into the street, headed north. I felt a blush of the alienness that keeps the visitor off balance everywhere. The traveler's dignity is always in peril. He knows that his speech, his clothes, his gestures are all out of place and slightly preposterous. The Cajuns understand and work to make the stranger comfortable.

I was stopped by a middle-aged man as I walked toward my car. He wore a fine cardigan sweater and a British-style touring cap. It was clear that he saw in me a fellow traveler, and less chance of making a fool of himself.

"Pardon me," he said in a cultivated accent from somewhere, "can you tell me where to buy boudin?"

I directed him to the grocery store half a block away, and told him he couldn't miss it. I also told him that he had come to the right place. Mamou, I said confidentially, makes the best boudin in the world.

South by Rail

Chicago could not have been grayer. It was eight o'clock in the morning and still barely daylight, so thick were the clouds. The travelers pulled their coats tight as they hurried through the dimness of Michigan Avenue's Central Station to get aboard the black and orange cars. They were nearly all Southerners, black expatriates headed home for the holidays, leaving behind for a little while the toils and pleasures of Chicago, the northernmost of the Southern outposts on the historic Illinois Central line, to refresh themselves in Port Gibson, Memphis, and the hundred other places they and their people sprang from.

Like all immigrants who yearn for the old country, these, too, must return home from time to time. Christmas is a favorite time. Some go by bus and some by automobile, but a great many still choose to go by the way they originally went up—on the aging coaches of the Illinois Central Railroad.

This is the great trunk line that ties together the northern and southern extremities of the nation's middle. When thousands of Negroes began to migrate from the oppressive agriculture of the South after the Civil War, it was largely the Illinois Central that delivered them to the industrial North, out of the bondage of Mississippi into the Promised Land of Illinois.

This band of pilgrims, as always, included those who remembered home and those who had never seen it. In one car rode Dr. John H. Mitchell, eighty-eight years old, a Chicago dentist for fifty-six years. He sat straight upright in his seat, polishing his ebony cane with his thumb as he talked of going for a visit to his boyhood home, Canton, Miss. In another car, Theodore Mims, five months old, was being carried to Drew, Miss., for the first time to be formally presented for the admiration of grandparents and uncles and loving aunts.

There were three or four hundred altogether, not so many as might ordinarily have gone on the last train before Christmas. An economic recession had cut the number. But, for the fortunate who were going, the anticipation was as keen as the first throb of a toothache. Children had been prepared for weeks. Even those too young to know the South firsthand seemed to feel the pull. A little way down the line, a conductor would come through a car shouting, "This way out to North Cairo," and a dark-eyed five-year-old beauty named Marva Crockett, who was making her first trip to Mississippi, would protest to the whole car, "I don't want to go to North Cairo. I want to go down South, right now!"

≈

The train pulled out at 8:05 a.m., away from the soot and overcoats of the city, and in less than an hour it was crawling through the flat, black land of Central Illinois, which, except for the red barns and neater houses, is so like the flat, brown land of the Mississippi Delta.

The club car was the first to melt the tensions of leave-taking. When the train crossed the Ohio River into Kentucky, just south of Cairo, an elderly man was so relaxed that he was able to sing for a laughing and appreciative audience, "Take me down to the river to be baptized!"

Dewitt Howard, twenty-eight years old, had begun drinking beer as soon as the train left Chicago. By ten a.m.

he was in a very friendly game of cards with a lonely woman traveler. At the other end of the club car four men also played cards as they drank, and from time to time one would draw a lucky card and purr, "How sweet it is."

Mr. Howard's older sister, Mrs. Laura Gaines, sat two cars forward with Marva Crockett, her stepdaughter. Mrs. Gaines, an ample woman who flashed gold with every smile, talked of the friends and kin she would see in Port Gibson, Miss., and of the Christmas dinner they would eat—ham, undoubtedly, and perhaps collard greens and almost certainly homemade muscadine wine.

The train stopped at Dyersburg and let off Stephanie Morris, eighteen, one of the few white persons on the trip. She was also one of the few true Northerners. She was a city person and, unlike the other travelers, was not happy to be going South. She was visiting friends, a kind of duty. "The South depresses me," she said.

Among the black Southerners, however, the Southern wrongs of the past seemed to be forgotten, at least for the holidays. Not a good word was heard about Chicago. Several spoke strongly of their dislike for the city. Mrs. Susie Williams said she knew several people who had moved back South.

"The North used to be the place to go," she said. "But now the South is going to be the North, and the North is going to be the South."

When Miss Morris got off, the train seemed to be left almost entirely to blacks, all of whom considered themselves Southern to some degree. Laughter and talk became freer as the train approached Memphis. A large group left there, and soon the Christmas lights were sparkling in the darkness of the Mississippi Delta.

Dewitt Howard, now switched to bourbon, got into a brief unpleasantness with a white conductor and a black porter over a cup of water he had spilled on the floor.

"I ain't never going to ride this train again," he said. He had already disclosed his plans. He was leaving Chicago after ten years of working in a sporting goods factory, putting laces in footballs, and was heading back to take over the family's forty-acre farm south of Port Gibson.

A second young woman had caught his eye in the club car. She was leaving Chicago for another reason. Her recent husband, whom she described as a notorious philanderer, had had the sour luck to catch her in a single indiscretion, and now was searching for her and was, she believed, going to kill her.

Mr. Howard pursued her vigorously and unsuccessfully. Finally, just north of Fulton, Ky., he proposed marriage to her. She rejected him, but not before he had told her, "I'll take you huntin' with me. I'll take you *fishin'*. There's a lake down there that's a *mile long*, and I've got a motorboat sittin' on that lake right now. You don't believe me? Come on home with me!"

Later, he talked once more of what he was leaving and what he was going home to. "I didn't like the life up there. You get up in the morning and you go to the factory and you do the same thing every day. Down here, I can get up when I please and do what I want to do."

He said he had been robbed about fifteen times in Chicago. "I ain't never been robbed in Mississippi."

His face clouded for a moment. "Lot of people out of work in Chicago. You go down by that employment office and there's long lines of people standing there, waiting."

Then he brightened. "My mother makes a garden. You can make it on a farm. I won't have nothing to worry about."

By mid-evening, south of Jackson, Mr. Howard had begun to pay court to another woman, and as the train moved past the low hills his voice talked and sang of how it would be when he reached the green, green grass of home.

The travelers were much diminished when the train crossed into Louisiana. It was nearly morning, very early, and a surprising number of those who were left were still awake, nursing their eighteen-hour weariness in the dark,

90

their heads pitching and rolling with the endless pitch and roll of the track.

Then the train moved into New Orleans, past the raised tombs of the first cemeteries, past the first of the raised cottages and gingerbread porches.

The porter who had angered Dewitt Howard relaxed at last. He sat down on one of the worn seats and, as the brakes squealed and the *City of New Orleans* came home to Christmas, began to sweet-talk a lonely and comely woman.

Blue Jerusalem

I drove to Texas one mild week in December to get myself a Christmas present. A few miles up the road from the town of Ben Wheeler, where I was headed, a couple of men in a cafe offered some firm opinions.

"All they're good for is eating feed," one of them said.

His companion disagreed. "They're good for breaking through your fence, too," he said.

I had confessed, over coffee, that I was on my way to get a burro. They advised me to think it over. I pressed on, though, and half a day later I was headed north with a young jack in the back of my truck.

The jack was dun-colored and Roman-nosed. It had the distinctive dark cross of the donkey down its back and withers. Riding down the highway, it seemed as absorbed as a child in the passing cars, the farmhouses, and the billboards advertising Jesus and Lone Star beer.

I named it Ben Wheeler in honor of the place where its life had been saved. Actually, it was saved at the Black Beauty Ranch, eight miles south of Ben Wheeler. But Black Beauty did not sound like a proper name for a donkey.

The ranch is run by the Fund for Animals, a New York-based animal rights organization that has rescued more than 7,000 wild burros that have been shoved off public lands in the West. Virtually all of the animals have been adopted as pets or as companions for horses and cattle.

Ben Wheeler was a Navy burro. He was in a herd of 4,000 burros that had been shipped to Texas from the China Lake Naval Weapons Center northeast of Los Angeles. They were in the way of the Navy's guns. Wild burros and horses are also a thorn in the side of Western ranchers who pay the government a nominal fee to run cattle and sheep on public lands. The wild animals compete for the sparse vegetation.

A few years ago, the government's policy was to shoot the wild burros and horses to thin the herds. Hundreds were killed. Others were shot for dog food by private hunters. Thousands of animals a year still face removal or, if a fragile bureaucracy of government and private efforts breaks down, slaughter.

When I was there, Black Beauty Ranch was managed by a Texan named Billy Jack Saxon. He, too, had firm opinions about burros.

"A burro makes a better pet than a dog," he said. We were walking through a herd of fifty or sixty. He called to a jenny named Friendly, and she nibbled open his palm, hoping perhaps to find an apple or a carrot. She cocked an ear and blinked when she was introduced to me.

Black Beauty Ranch is a haven not only for burros but also for abused animals of many kinds. A horse that had been shot in the leg by an angry owner in Georgia was brought in the day I arrived. About five hundred wild goats that the Fund had rescued from San Clemente Island (the Navy was going to shoot them) were grazing in one of the pastures. Wild hogs from the same place were rooting contentedly.

Nim Chimpsky, a chimpanzee that learned sign language and enjoyed brief television fame several years ago, lives at Black Beauty. He shares quarters with a female named Sally. Mr. Saxon told me that Nim had been rescued from a drug experiment that would finally have killed him.

The Fund for Animals, which is headed by the writer Cleveland Amory, has defended whales, seals, dolphins, impounded dogs and cats, laboratory mice and other victims of what the organization sees as human cruelty and neglect. The Texas ranch is one of its main projects. Mr. Amory began buying the acreage in 1980, and when I was there he had accumulated six hundred acres of rolling grassland. The place was dotted with pines and ponds. The fence was whitewashed. The barns were sturdy and clean. Three young employees were grinding grain in a mechanized mill and filling feed troughs. Some of the young burros studied the mill like teenagers looking over an old car.

The Spanish brought burros to the New World four hundred years ago. In North America, most have become desert creatures. These latest immigrants, after a noisy roundup and a 1,500-mile journey, find themselves in East Texas facing a lushness of greenery that must seem strange and wonderful. The pastures are bordered by woods and creeks. Perhaps there is such a place in the folk memory of those whose ancestors came from the brighter geography of Europe. Those descended from places like North Africa and the Near East, and whose progenitors here have known nothing more pleasing than sagebrush and cactus, are surely stunned into disbelief when they step off the truck at Black Beauty Ranch.

A new load comes in from the desert once or twice a month. The Fund's old tractor-trailer chugs down the main street of Ben Wheeler, past the cafe and Booster Moore's general store and on down Farm-to-Market Road 773 to the ranch. After a few days of attention and good hay, the new arrivals begin to take an interest in their surroundings. They seem to understand that something promising is in the wind.

The ranch is supposed to be a way station. Most go on to adoption centers elsewhere. But a few invariably are too old or too sick to move. They stay on, sharing the pastures with broken-down race horses, old circus animals, and other creatures that have been rescued from one difficulty or another. When I was there, the burros varied in age from long-eared colts to toothless beasts past thirty. One of the permanent residents was a white jack named Al, who was thought to be nearly forty years old. "He hasn't got a tooth in his head," Mr. Saxon said.

Mr. Amory told me that of the 7,000 burros that the Fund had put out for adoption, fewer than five had been sent back. Most people treat them as pets. Some train them to carry riders and pull carts. My burro's career is still undecided. So far, he has made himself useful only as a kind of baby-sitter for the young calves. He runs with the cattle, and when a new one is born he immediately intrudes himself into the youngster's affections. He first checks it over like a veterinarian, then, when it is strong enough to walk and run, he nudges and chases it back and forth in the tall grass. The mothers are annoyed, but they have not found a way to stop him.

Authorities on the donkey (the English word for burro) say the animal is more intelligent than the horse. That reputation, however, may be a triumph of public relations. The donkey has exceptional ears, which suggest alertness, and large brown eyes that seem to reflect dry wit and some hidden wisdom. The donkey is also blessed with an extremely fast spring-action in the rear legs, which it uses occasionally to support a sense of dignity.

The ass has always carried man's burdens, some more important than others. Mr. Amory told me that he once pulled a "tremendously fat" man off a donkey's back in Morocco, and nearly caused a riot. Donkeys of perhaps the same blood lines carried Jesus into Jerusalem and Mary into Bethlehem.

On the way home from Texas, I learned by chance that the dun, cross-bearing burro like Ben Wheeler has a special designation. We were about twenty miles from Hogeye. I stopped to ask directions on a narrow dirt road, and the farmer came out to look over the burro. He noted the dark stripes of the cross and the desert-gray coat.

95

"They call this a Blue Jerusalem mule," he said. "It's the kind that Mary was riding."

The burro looked sage. He seemed to be speculating that, with a little luck, he would spend the rest of his Christmases in a dry barn eating alfalfa hay, with occasional visits from a couple of old men who enjoy the company of mules.

Hurricanes and
Other Temptations

My first recollection of New Orleans is of a whiff of danger.
A bartender served me an illegal mint julep when I was
seventeen. Years later, I learned that New Orleans barten-
ders don't see anything wrong with serving strong drink to
youngsters. I have seen waiters there set wineglasses in
front of children when they dine out with their parents.

The South Louisiana attitude toward alcohol is one reason the city is considered dangerous in the glum precincts
of the Upper South where I come from. Generations of
Baptists have stolen down there to put their souls at risk on
the sly. In all the years since my first wickedness there,
I have never quite shaken free of a thrilling apprehension
when I am in New Orleans. I now know that even those
who live beyond the Bible Belt, in what we call The North,
recognize the same attraction. People are drawn to the
place by the chance that something will happen to them.

Geography is responsible for much of the lurid appeal.
Sieur de Bienville, the city's founder, chose the site to establish French control of the central Gulf Coast, the mouth
of the Mississippi, and as much as possible of the river's
watershed. The river mouth itself was an unstable marsh,
so he had to travel a hundred miles upriver to find land dry
enough to build a town on. Bienville would have saved suc-
ceeding generations a lot of trouble if he had gone another
hundred.

Much of the city is below sea level. That means that the most important people in town are the men who run the water pumps. Without the pumps, large expanses of the old city and several entire suburbs would be under water during the wet seasons. The city would look, from the air, as Lake Pontchartrain would look if it were planted with rows of red-tiled roofs.

The Mississippi River, which spreads this threat across the Louisiana delta, is the most interesting continuous drama in New Orleans. The Mississippi does not plunge straight south into the Gulf of Mexico. It begins to curve about Baton Rouge, then flattens out and heads due east. It whips through New Orleans in an eastering series of sharp bends, like a cottonmouth moccasin striking at Mobile, and finally, a few miles below the city, curves back to the south and flows solemnly into the Gulf as if it had never intended anything else.

When I lived in New Orleans, some years ago, I spent many sunny hours on the river bank. One Sunday after-noon in the spring I was walking on the levee at the foot of Carrollton Avenue. The river was near flood stage. Green trees swept past, and driftwood nudged into the eddies and occasionally lodged on the bank. The shipyards on the opposite shore were quiet but tankers and barge tows churned along the river highway. Behind me, and several feet below the surface of the penned-in river, lay rows and streets of Caribbean houses—airy, high-ceilinged, gal-leried, gingerbreaded—waiting out one more spring to see whether the river would burst through and sweep them off their feet.

I noticed a string of barges moored on the bank, tied to trees and stakes. I stood for some time wondering whether the current might break the cables. I suppose that I secretly yearned to see the barges snap free.

A day or two later, *The Times-Picayune* reported that a string of barges had broken their moorings on the bank. Twelve or fifteen of them had bobbed and whirled in the

98

direction of the Greater New Orleans Bridge, and one or two had struck ships, before the tugboats had caught them. A tugboat captain works on the edge of danger, and in a stampede he must have the nerve of a gunfighter.

The river seems to stir a restlessness in the inhabitants of New Orleans. On countless days I have gone to the Carrollton levee or to the river walk opposite Jackson Square looking for a few minutes of quiet, and have found something else instead. Other residents used to tell me they had the same experience.

The river is never quiet. A visitor from the inland might think that the ships are moving up and down in peace. But New Orleanians know that at the wheel of every vessel is a pilot who never relaxes, or does so at great peril. A few years ago, just up the river at Luling, the pilot of a ferry relaxed one morning. He was drinking, and steered his boat into the path of a Norwegian tanker. Seventy-seven people died.

The river kills people every year. You can hear the stories in the foreign sailors' bars on Decatur Street, downstairs from the clubs where the Middle Eastern belly dancers work. Decatur is one of the last streets in the French Quarter to be gentrified. Interspersed among clean, sandblasted brick walls and freshly painted courtyards are long blocks of dingy old stucco buildings. The smells of the Quarter are usually of food—sauces simmering, bread baking, coffee beans roasting. But along Decatur, the street nearest the river, the air suspiring from a rotting stairwell or the open door of a bar smells a hundred years old.

Another piece of the waterfront that captivates me is the Canal Street ferry. It runs to old Algiers, which is now part of New Orleans but used to be a separate town for people who wanted a little distance between themselves and the urban confusion, or between themselves and the law. Store clerks and office workers live there now and use the ferry.

There are two or three old-fashioned bars near the Algiers landing, and my excuse for riding the ferry is to visit one of them. The real reason, though, is more sinister. The ferry must be nimble to thread its way through the ship traffic. I ride the ferry for the same reason that I used to cover vigilante mobs in Selma and I.R.A. guerrillas in Belfast. Something is always happening, or about to happen.

The whole city lives on the verge of events. The day I moved there, I stumbled onto an impromptu parade. A marching band emerged from the close shadows and wrought-iron balconies of Royal Street, commandeered half of broad Canal Street and headed toward the river playing Dixieland jazz. People along the sidewalks fell in behind and danced along, strutting and grinning. We were hypnotized. Some hollered for joy, like celebrants at a Pentecostal revival. I had the feeling that if the band had chosen to march over the edge of the dock, all of us, black and white together, would have followed happily, right into the Mississippi.

There is a secret wildness in New Orleans beneath the summer humidity and autumn lassitude. The main source of it is nature, which is as close as the brackish tides that encroach on the very suburbs. The people of the city understand that their petty divisions could be swept away in an hour if the river levee should give way. If a hurricane of the proper force should strike the city at the proper angle, Lake Pontchartrain would wash across the city like coffee sloshed into a saucer. Catastrophe aside, the city lives every day with the imposing power of subtropical climate. The delta sun in August will drive the hardiest fool indoors.

But nature is not the whole story. New Orleans straddles a cultural fault that is as ominous as the San Andreas. At just this point, where the Mississippi is almost home, two differing peoples and points of view come up against each other and occupy the same territory.

In the simplest terms, the two cultures are the Roman

Catholic and the Protestant, descendants of the eighteenth-century Creole settlers, French and Spanish speaking, and the nineteenth-century Americans who came down the river from the English-speaking states.

A. J. Liebling, in *The Earl of Louisiana,* perceived Louisiana as the westernmost Arab state, an extension of the quarrelsome Levant. Walker Percy, who writes from the northern shore of Lake Pontchartrain, chooses to emphasize coexistence. He has described Baton Rouge, the state capital, as a model of cultural cooperation: politicians looting the state with Protestant industry and Catholic gaiety.

I lean toward Mr. Percy's view. In my seven years as a resident of New Orleans, I saw little open conflict between Protestants and Catholics and only slightly more between whites and blacks. There was some resentment against the oil company newcomers from Texas, many of whom would approach no closer than the western suburbs and seemed fearful of the mysterious, polyglot center of the city.

But the newcomers, like the riverboat Kaintucks 150 years ago, will eventually lose their anxieties and give in to the delta pace, just as the French did, and the Africans, and the Spanish, and the Sicilians. A little way up the river are the descendants of old German families with names like Schexnayder; the grandparents speak the same twangy, redneck French as the descendants of the Acadians.

Now and then, someone resists the pace. William Faulkner lived in New Orleans in 1925. He escaped back to Mississippi, and probably forfeited a life of ease. He might still be alive today, idly eyeballing the Haspel suits and dark-eyed women from a borrowed room on Pirate's Alley.

The city makes it easy to give in by pretending to be lazy, laid-back and unconcerned. Its motto is "The City That Care Forgot." Someone is rehearsing for Mardi Gras every day in some corner of the town. Magazine Street, which has become an outpost of Central America, parties on Saturday night in Spanish. Jackson Square parties every day at noon in English, set to music. When a businessman tires of his office, he takes lunch in Jackson Square and listens to the freelance singers and guitar players.

The square is self-catering. You buy a muffuletta sandwich at the Central Grocery, a block away, and walk back to the square with the store's mist of olive oil, garlic and Italian cheese in your head. Then you choose a bench in the sun if it is December, January or February and in the shade in all other seasons. The benches all face the statue of General Jackson and his rearing horse.

I have occasionally been invited to the balcony of one or another of the Pontalba apartments, which face the square and look off toward St. Louis Cathedral. From the balcony, the various strains of music mingle with the easy conversation of the strollers and sidewalk artists, and it is difficult at such times to remember that nature lives in the same park. But I have also been in Jackson Square on the day after a hurricane, and have seen the crape myrtles slashed and uprooted.

New Orleans is never more dangerous, or more alluring, than during a hurricane. A good storm takes days to arrive from the Gulf, and the anticipation of it wholly invigorates the city. People watch the sky. It turns hard blue as the wind begins to rise, then whitens for a while and casts a false, dreadful light on everything below. Just before the worst the sky darkens, and finally, ink-black and full of weight, it collapses in fury and the wind binds it to the land and water.

My first hurricane was Betsy, in the fall of 1965. It arrived at New Orleans in the evening. The street lights shattered and people huddled indoors in candlelight. Some flitted from house to house for a drink with the neighbors— a last drink, in some cases. Hurricane parties are a tradition on the Gulf Coast. Four years after Betsy, several dozen people in an apartment house at Pass Christian, Miss., went to their death toasting the hurricane of the century, Camille.

Betsy's visitors who had not, to their secret delight, got out of town in time drifted together for informal parties in the downtown hotels. Jack Nelson of *The Los Angeles Times* and I were there to cover a civil rights trial in Federal Court, and had got caught. We spent the worst of the storm in the Touché Bar on the lower level of the Royal Orleans Hotel. The front door was lined with sandbags to keep the rainwater out. A woman named Monique played the piano and sang cabaret songs for half a dozen men who pretended to be lonely. Metal signs, garbage cans and broken glass clattered down Royal Street most of the night.

I went upstairs to bed about midnight. Jack made a last walk through the hotel lobby and stopped to chat with an auxiliary policeman who had stepped into the dry for a moment. As they stood in the doorway, they were startled to see a young woman running and screaming down the middle of Royal Street. The policeman grabbed her and pulled her into the lobby. When she got her wits back, she told a story that the two men found incredible. She had gone out to buy milk for the baby, she said (dressed improbably in stockings and a cocktail dress), and on the way back two men had accosted her, dragged her under a tree on the lawn of the federal courthouse, and tried to rape her. Jack and the policeman noticed that she was barefoot; that was the only evidence that she might be telling the truth.

The policeman remembered some other duty and asked Jack to see after the woman. In the blinding rain and hundred-mile-an-hour wind, they struggled down the street to the familiar magnolia tree on the courthouse lawn. There, to Jack's amazement, they found her purse and shoes. He escorted her home to what sounded, from the top of the stairs, like an anxious and angry husband. Jack left hurriedly, and marveled all the way back to the hotel on the mysterious eroticism of an act of God.

I learned later that while Jack and I were sitting safely in the Touché Bar, and while the young woman in evening wear was braving the storm for the baby's milk, an aging man named George Rojas was clinging to the top of a light pole a few miles down the river. He stayed there five hours with a rope around his waist, watching trees, barrels and drowned animals whirl past in the water at his feet.

He was still shaken two days afterward as he told me of having twice been knocked off the pole and of painfully drawing himself back by the rope. He finally had cast himself loose to help a man save his wife and four children, and they all had made their way somehow to a sand dredge to wait out the storm. Sixty-two other people who were caught out that night did not survive.

After the hurricane, in the sunlit wreckage, George Rojas had become a rare kind of Louisianian—a convert to good sense. "I wouldn't have give a penny for myself," he said. He vowed never again to stay in town when the weathermen urged everybody to head north.

Two or three more hurricanes, including the killer Camille, struck the Louisiana and Mississippi coasts after I went to New Orleans to live. I never left town for any of them. I would bet my life savings that George Rojas did not, either. I can tell you what was in his mind. He figured that, if he left, he might miss something.

Vernon McCall
and the Government

The story ended in early June. I remember, the day before, hearing the call of an ovenbird in the deepening green of the woods. I had met Vernon McCall earlier in the week, and when I heard the ovenbird I was tempted to think of it as a metaphor for Vernon. Like the ovenbird, Vernon was small and shy. He seemed to suffer at being seen. But the metaphor failed finally because the little bird, for all its secretiveness, was thoroughly outspoken. When it flew up from the leaves and mold to proclaim its territory, it sang out with a volume and assertiveness that even crows would respect.

The McCall clan made up more than half of the hundred or so families in an isolated Blue Ridge valley called Balsam Grove, N.C. The other McCalls were true mountaineers: tall, lean, sturdy, pale-eyed, wry-humored, close-mouthed, quick to take offense. Vernon was different. He was short, stooped, diabetic, and epileptic. He spoke softly and he trusted strangers, perhaps because, in his frailty, he had no choice.

It was this forty-year-old waif who turned out to be the principal target when the United States government chose to exert its authority in Transylvania County. The trouble blew into the open one winter day when the government destroyed Vernon's home. But it had been building for a year before that.

The people of the Carolina mountains once considered the United States Forest Service to be their friend. The residents of Balsam Grove figured they had better be friendly because they were surrounded. Their community was a dot in the middle of the huge Pisgah National Forest. There had been years of peaceful coexistence. The McCalls and their neighbors had avoided the old mountain custom of burning the woods, and in return the government had blinked most of the time when the residents hunted and fished illegally in the federally protected woods.

But about a year earlier, the Forest Service, which looked after the National Forest, ended the policy of live and let live. It began sending surveyors onto the private property adjoining the National Forest to recheck old property lines. In more than a year of resurveying, the government had not found a single error in a private property owner's favor. Land that had been used for years as pasture and cropland was now said to be an encroachment on federal property. The disputed strips varied from a few feet wide to many yards.

The government's methods did not help matters. On one wooded tract, a surveyor ran a line, painted a row of trees to mark it, then decided he had made a mistake. He sawed down the painted trees and ran a second line. Once again he had erred, and that row of trees was cut. He finally settled on a third line. The Forest Service never offered to pay the landowner for the cut trees.

Then, in the midst of the resurveying, the government began the controversial practice of clear-cutting in the National Forest. Various members of the McCall clan showed me half a dozen patches of mountainside that had been peeled of every bush, balsam, and hardwood, then bulldozed, to prepare the cleared land for planting white pine seedlings. I saw a hundred-acre mountain top that had been stripped to the red clay subsoil. It was visible for miles from the high, winding roads.

106

Richard McCall, one of Balsam Grove's leaders, and one of Vernon's cousins, took me on a tour on the next to last day of my visit. He drove first down a steep dirt road and stopped to gaze into a wooded draw that had not been molested by the government. The oaks reached up more than a hundred feet and many were fifteen to eighteen inches in diameter at the trunk. It was here that I heard the ovenbird. Its sharp call rose up from the dark floor of the hollow, up through the sunlight's spots and out the roof of the oaks. Richard McCall acknowledged the bird only by waiting for it to finish singing. Then he told me about the woods.

"This was cut over the last time about fifty years ago. It took it this long to get back like this."

Then he drove half a mile down the road and stopped beside a clear-cut patch. The trees and saplings, even the wild azaleas, rhododendrons and mountain laurel bushes, their blooms wilted, were lying in brown piles. "They're just about to ruin this country, the way I see it," Mr. McCall said.

Fishermen were angry. The spring rains had washed red clay into the creeks. Hunters were angry. "Can't nothing live in a pine thicket—deer, squirrels, not nothing," Spurgeon McCall, another cousin of Vernon, told me.

Spurgeon was one of Balsam Grove's angriest young men. He was an unrepentant violator of the game laws. He had served time in the federal penitentiary for his repeated incursions on the National Forest, and he swore to me that he would continue to hunt there if they did not cut it all down.

During the growing hostility between Balsam Grove and the government, the Forest Service made its move against Vernon McCall. The agency decided that the one-acre tract that his house trailer sat on, in a woods with the mountains rising in the background, was legally part of Pisgah National Forest. It sent a letter that January to Cannon McCall, Vernon's 89-year-old father, who claimed ownership of the acre, and warned him to take everything off the property by February 22. The father did not respond.

Vernon was away from home much of the day February 22. He lived alone. He had no regular employment. He worked at odd jobs in the winter, and in the warm months he picked and sold blackberries and sprigs of mountain laurel. For whatever reason, he was not there when the district forest ranger arrived with eight workmen and a bulldozer.

Finding the trailer locked, they broke in and removed a bed and two or three other items of furniture and set them down in the mud outside. Then they dug a large hole with the bulldozer and shoved the trailer in and covered it up. Vernon also had a small barn, a hog pen and a wooden milk box over the spring that provided his water. They buried those, too.

An angry crowd of neighbors gathered, but the ranger and his workmen went on with the job. "My orders came from Atlanta, and this property must be cleared before we leave here," the ranger told Cannon McCall.

Spurgeon McCall was still furious when I talked to him in June. I found him in his front yard working on a machine. His jeans and shirt were dirty. He wore a felt hat with the band cut away to make it look like a skull cap. His face was lean, his hair was dark, and his sideburns were long. He stood in a slouch and looked me in the eye.

Spug, as his friends called him, had gone to Vernon's place that day with Glenn McCall, one of Vernon's brothers. They found Vernon in the crowd. He had returned in time to see his trailer pushed into the hole, Spug recalled.

"Vernon was sittin' under a tree lookin' dazed. The ranger walks up to Glenn, says, 'Glenn, I hope there ain't no hard feelin's over this.' Glenn didn't answer, just looked at the ground.

"He come over to me. 'Spug, ain't no hard feelin's, is

108

there?' And I says, 'Well, you just went and buried a man's dwellin' place. It had everything in it belonged to his dead mama and his two dead brothers. Then you knocked down his barn and hog pen and buried them, too. What you figger you got to do to cause hard feelin's—piss in a feller's face?'"

The community was enraged. For weeks, the young men talked of taking guns to the Forest Service men. When I arrived in June there was still talk of setting fire to the National Forest. "It's a wonder they didn't get this country burnt down," Spug told me.

The only McCall who did not get angry, as far as I could tell, was Vernon. The destruction of his home had a different effect on him. "Vernon's bad to drink," Mrs. Leonard Griffin, whose family gave me bed and board, told me just before the end, "and he's been drinking a lot more since they buried his trailer."

Vernon's friends had set up another trailer for him on the highway right-of-way in front of the disputed acre. He had ventured back onto the land that the Forest Service claimed to plow a garden and plant six rows of potatoes. He showed me the potatoes, and then he showed me a bowl of plastic flowers that he had placed on the grave of his old trailer. He mentioned mementoes of his mother and the two brothers that lay buried underneath. Mrs. Griffin had told me about the brothers. They had frozen to death beside a whiskey still in 1970.

Vernon's speech, like his body, was slow. He and I walked ponderously around the place. He called back memories with what seemed like physical effort. We stopped beside the spring and he pointed to pieces of his milk box that the workmen had missed.

With some pride, he said, "I kept milk and butter both in there."

I saw him on Friday. On Saturday, just at nightfall, he and three younger men from another community were

109

walking along state highway 215, drinking whiskey.

A quarrel began. A passing motorist saw blows being struck.

Another car came along a few seconds later. The driver saw something in the middle of the highway but in the dimness realized too late that it was two men, lying crosswise.

The younger man escaped. Vernon, as usual, did not. He was killed.

I left the next day. I drove past the government's little acre and found it quiet. I noticed, however, that the government agents, when they should come again to claim their land, would have to move not only Vernon's potato plants but also his chair, which he had left sitting under a shade tree noticeably over the property line.

The Bloody English

Four hundred thousand of the two million people in my home state claim English ancestry. The figure comes from a rather fuzzy calculation in the 1980 census. I am suspicious of it. My own ancestors (according to a family tradition that is at least as uncertain as the census) were Scotch-Irish, a race despised by the English as having the worst blood of both islands. My guess is that most of Arkansas's English are not English at all but transmogrified Scotch-Irish. Hugh Kenner, the critic and writer, observed while visiting Dublin a few years ago that in Ireland a fact does not have the same specific gravity that it has in more sedate countries. The northern Irish Protestants, those we call the Scotch-Irish when they come on to America, have at least that in common with the hated southern Catholics; they are all liars.

Aside from snobbery, though, the only motive I can think of for a Scotch-Irish Arkansawyer's lying about his ancestry is not wanting to be identified with the Protestant killers and bigots who, along with the Catholic I.R.A., are giving Ulster a bad name today. Who wants anything to do with a people whose most inspiring contemporary leader is the Rev. Ian Paisley?

In the interest of improving the self-image of the Scotch-Irish, I want to say a few words about the English. I lived

111

among the English for two years. If the Scotch-Irish are big-oted and bad-tempered, their cousins across the Irish Sea are arrogant, lazy, class-ridden, racist, and bloody-minded. That last is what the English call each other. It means blink-ered and deliberate ignorance, or aggressive unconcern for what anyone else thinks.

During the time I lived in England, hardly a day went by that I did not find some reason to curse an Englishman. The first time I went to Dublin on business, I was pleased to learn that the English currency in my pocket was as ac-ceptable in Irish stores as Irish currency. But the English did not return the favor. When I got back to London, I absent-mindedly handed over an Irish penny with some English pennies at a ticket counter on the Underground. The clerk shoved it back at me—literally shoved it—and snapped, "This is no good here." I gave him a piece of my mind, and was immediately sorry, because I knew that he would add my outburst to his list of reasons for despising Americans. If the English are arrogant, bloody-minded, etc., Americans are ignorant, loud, insensitive and boor-ish; any Englishman will tell you that.

I was thinking of all this some time ago after I heard that some American friends were spending the summer in an English village. I happened to know the village, a farm-ing settlement east of Cambridge, and suddenly I longed to be there. All my surliness fell away as I remembered a time that my wife and I had spent in the same village. I had an urge to sell a cow and fly over to join them.

What is it about the English that makes them so easy to forgive? I don't care to bog down in a quest for their na-tional character—some Arkansas *Englishman* can tackle that—but I have a few thoughts about a special English in-stitution that may shed light on the question. The insti-tution happens to be one that we could use in Arkansas—the pub.

I am speaking of the village pub, because that is what

all pubs essentially are, even those in the heart of London. And therein lies the value of a pub: it is the main institution that ties neighbor to neighbor everywhere in England. In earlier times, the church was the center of every community. But the English are no longer very religious, and the pub has become the one institution that no English community—whether village or city neighborhood—can comfortably do without.

A perception of quaintness has almost ruined the pub for Americans. Every American writer who visits England sends back tales of the antique tables and the warm beer and the funny pub names. Pubs become so precious that Americans want nothing to do with them, except as exotica to be sampled along with castles and kidney pie when they go to England as tourists.

The truth about pubs is much homelier. The pub is simply a place to see the neighbors, catch up on the news, and relax until bedtime. For all their national arrogance and contempt for their fellowman, the English like to be with their friends after dinner. They don't go to the pub every night, but they feel that one or two visits a week add regularity to their lives.

In Radwinter, the Essex village where Norma and I spent a week some years ago, our cottage was next door to that of a retired farm worker named Gerald Bacon. Mr. Bacon was a pillar of Radwinter's Anglican Church—served on committees, rang the bells, mowed the grass. He was also a pillar of the Red Lion. He went there every Friday night, just as he went to church every Sunday morning. That was part of the rhythm of the week. He went to market in Saffron-Walden, five miles away, every Tuesday, because Tuesday had been market day in Saffron-Walden for a hundred years. The fishmonger always came to Radwinter on Wednesday. Bell-ringing, a kind of musical sport, was Sunday evening at six, and Mr. Bacon was always in the tower to call the changes and pull the rope with his friends.

113

With the same regularity, he walked down the Old Roman Road to the Red Lion every Friday after dinner, and drank beer.

He did not drink to get drunk. He nursed one pint all evening and would have been mortified if he had got drunk. The purpose of drinking beer in a pub is to socialize, catch up on the news and relax. Mr. Bacon knew that he could depend on finding the same beer, the same faces and pretty much the same news every Friday evening. Nothing ever happened to distort the rhythm of the week. Not often, anyway. A few years ago, the publican's wife ran off with a salesman and that caused a tremor in the village pulse. But she recovered her senses and came home. She went back to waiting tables, and life continued as before.

Americans are sometimes puzzled by the English attitude toward drunkenness. I know a bar in Fayetteville where they expect a killing every year and a serious fight every Saturday night, because getting drunk is what the customers come for. The only Arkansas bar I know that frowns on drunkenness is Roger's Pool Hall at Fayetteville. Someone occasionally slips over the line (there was a famous brawl a few years ago that threatened to eliminate the entire creative writing program at the University), but most of Roger's customers would be at home in the Red Lion Pub at Radwinter, allowing for intolerance, boorishness, and other national frailties.

Roger's customers might balk at warm beer. The English are insistent—you might say bloody-minded—on the subject of temperature. They believe that chilling beer kills the taste. Warm or chilled, beer is essential to a pub, and not just to warm the feelings and keep conversation going. One of the problems with our own village gathering places is the beverages served. West Fork, a small town near Hogeye, has a cafe that is the rough equivalent of an English pub. The town is dry, so no beer is served. People go there in the evenings to chat, catch up on the news—and drink coffee. Those who don't like coffee drink Coke or Pepsi. All of it is full of caffeine and sugar. Instead of going in after dinner and relaxing, people go in and tighten up. By bedtime, some of those old Baptists are flying as high as Scheduled Skyways.

The English are intensely loyal to their pub. Radwinter has three. Each has its steady clientele, as each of the three churches has. I think one reason the English distrust Americans is because we do not settle on a single drinking place and stick with it. Gerald Bacon would not think of drinking beer anywhere except at the Red Lion. He has drunk there all his life, as did his father, who was also a farm worker.

The deepest loyalty, of any kind, that I encountered in England was at another Radwinter pub, Mrs. Digby's. (No one expected constancy from me; I went to all of them.) I walked down to Mrs. Digby's alone after dinner one night. The English, arrogant and condescending though they are, go out of their way to be friendly to American visitors. So I was not surprised when a middle-aged woman next to me on the bench struck up a conversation. After a few minutes, it occurred to me, from her fluttering eyelids and coquettish vowels, that she was not merely making conversation. I began to construct an identity for her: here was a lonely widow, down at the pub with her son, and she thought she might pick up a safe stranger for the evening.

And the young man with her, who was at least twenty years younger than she, surely must be her son, or perhaps a nephew. He joined the conversation and the three of us spent an entertaining hour discussing the warmth of British-American relations and other pleasant topics. Then closing time was announced and the two of them got up to leave.

The young man said, "It's been lovely, but my wife and I really must be going. We live in the next village, and it's a four-mile walk."

115

Mainly to cover my astonishment, I said, "You walk four miles to a pub?"

"Oh, yes," he said. "Our village doesn't have a pub. We walk over to Mrs. Digby's three or four nights a week."

The last I saw of them they were striding off down the Old Roman Road at about ten miles an hour, holding hands.

A Letter to
My Great-Grandfather

You may wonder, Mitch, why I'm writing to a man who's been dead longer than I have been alive. The reason is that you're the oldest member of the family that we know. When something important happens, the head of the family ought to be told. I have a piece of news, and I will tell you about it in a minute. But it's not the kind of news that you will enjoy, so before I get into that, let me bring you up to date on what's happened since you died. Calvin Coolidge was President then, and a lot has changed. I'm not going into all that has happened around the United States; that's too much of a mess to explain to a man of 150. But I will try to report on what's happened closer to home.

For instance, I happen to know that you were interested in politics, at least in Yell County politics. We have advanced very far, politically. Yell County is now represented in the Legislature by a man who knows all there is to know about India. Some fool wanted to send a bunch of professors to India to see why the women had so many babies, and our man put a stop to it. He could tell from here what caused them to have babies.

I think you were interested in religion, too. What I have to tell you about religion will amaze you. Some of the richest men in America now are preachers. Arkansas hasn't got many rich ones yet, although we have shouldered our part of the load to make them rich in Oklahoma and California. But the best part of it, Mitch, is that any old ordinary Baptist nowadays owns a brick house, two cars and a pickup truck. And he owes it all to the Lord. That's how advanced we have become in theology.

You will also be interested to hear what has happened between men and women. I know that you outlived two wives and nearly outlived a third one, even though she was twenty years younger than you. I don't know how to tell you this, but husbands don't outlive their wives any more. Not even the hillbillies.

I visited your grave at Aly not long ago. You will be glad to know that it's in good shape. The living always assume that the dead are concerned about that sort of thing. It occurs to me that you might never have heard what they inscribed on your tombstone. It says:

> Corpl. Mitchel Reed
> Co. A
> 4 Ark. Cav.

I can't help wondering how you feel being remembered for all time as a soldier. There were any number of other possibilities: Farmer. Deacon in the Baptist Church. Member of the School Board. Loving Father and Husband (of three different women).

And being remembered not just as a soldier, Mitch, but as a Union soldier. I know that Yell County had mixed opinions about the war, but you had to know that a Union veteran would not have much of a future in Arkansas, even in the Ouachita Mountains. I've never understood why you went back to Yell County after the armistice. My guess is that it had something to do with Cynthia. I see by her tombstone that she was just twenty-three when you buried her. That's about all we know about her.

> Cynthia, wife of M. Reed
> Born Mar. 27, 1838
> Died Nov. 23, 1861

That, and a little scrap of verse:

> Here lies all our beloved and best
> We leave the dear sleeper with her God to rest

You and I never knew each other, Mitch, and the family's memory of you was a little thin by the time I was old enough to understand about ancestors. By now, you have pretty well shaded into the larger community. I guess it is impertinent to presume a friendship between two men when one of them has been dead for nearly sixty years and the two of them are connected by not much more than a tombstone and a cranky old mantel clock. I don't see much of the tombstone, but the clock sits upstairs and strikes the time at the beginning of every hour. Sometimes it wakes me up in the middle of the night just to remind me that I wouldn't be here if it hadn't been for you.

About this piece of news I have for you—I've been trying to figure out why it's news. I've spent most of my life in the news business, and we were always taught that news is some development that's timely or close at hand, or important. This little item that I have for you does not really qualify on any count. I said it was important, but it does not seem like much when I remember that the quarrel has been going on four hundred years. And that four hundred years is just the time that we, our family, have been involved in it. The historians say that it has actually been under way for eight hundred years.

We, our family, could have stayed out of it if the English kings had not lured our old Scotch daddies to Ireland. We had never had much use for Catholics, but I don't think we got excited about the threat from Rome until they sent us to Ireland to work the plantations. The best way to learn to hate somebody is to take his land away from him. So in a very short time we had learned to hate the Catholics, and they had learned to hate us, and we had both learned to hate the English. That may not be accurate history, Mitch,

119

but it is what the poets tell us, and we all know that poetry is stronger than history.

After we came on over to Carolina and Virginia, we more or less made peace with the English, excepting one or two incidents. But we never forgot how to hate the Catholics. Mitch, I can remember when I was a boy hearing the preachers in our family get up in the pulpit and use the same words on the Catholics that they used on the Devil. I was nearly grown before I was able to walk past the Catholic Church at Hot Springs without shivering. I'm sure you grew up with the same feeling, but you at least had an idea where the feeling came from. You were still close to the source. I was a grown man before I figured out that the hatred came from Ulster. We brought it over with us in our Scotch-Irish blood, and nourished it through eight or ten generations when none of us ever laid eyes on a Catholic, and across wilderness and hills where even the Baptists were scarce.

Mitch, I have a theory that I wish I could talk over with you. Most of our family have been Baptists going back at least to your generation, and probably before that. I wish I could shift over to 1884 and sit down with you and ask a few questions. You were settling in and making a place for yourself in Yell County about that time. I reckon you would have been one of the squires of the community—a war veteran, head of a family, a reasonably prosperous farmer as prosperity was measured in the hills of Arkansas during Reconstruction. What I would like to know is this: Who kept the peace in Aly, Arkansas, in 1884? You were at least a day's ride from the county seat at Danville. I suppose you had a local constable, but one man could not do much to impose the law on a wild place at the end of the road.

Mitch, I don't think that we, my generation, are going to understand who we are until we own up to who you were. And I figure that you were just about two generations away from the woods. I don't mean any offense, but *your* great-grandfather had to be practically a savage.

Not that you could blame him. His people had got off the boat in Charleston or one of those high-toned places, and headed west up the first river. Lived in the woods in the summer and huddled under a lean-to in the winter. Took up with the first gal he met and she probably not more than fourteen. May or may not have bothered to register the marriage. We've figured out from some of the evidence that a lot of the transplanted Ulstermen swapped wives the way they swapped horses once they got out of sight of civilization. They lived so far back in the wilderness that the preachers couldn't follow them.

Then after a while the rough edges smoothed away and the preachers lit out for the hills and caught up with them. And here is my theory, Mitch: The main thing that kept the peace in the Southern backwoods was not the law but the church. The Baptist Church, especially, because that was the one that traveled lightest. The Baptists were full of fire and would go anywhere. The Anglicans—well, you couldn't expect a bishop to live in a place where he couldn't get his tablecloth ironed. But the Baptist preachers knew how to eat with their fingers, and that gave them the moral authority to deal with men and women who lived in a state of nature.

Mitch, I think we've got to admit that the people who came ahead of us—not just our family, but all those thousands of Scotch-Irishmen who learned to hate and fight at the knees of the best haters and eye-gougers the world has ever known—that these ancestors of ours simply were not civilized. Some people say that the Southern Indians were barbarians. Hell, Mitch, a lot of the Indians were settled people—farmers, some of them were, with laws and rules and religious codes. They must have looked at us the same way the Europeans looked at Genghis Khan. We were the invaders. And we were barbarians, especially after a couple of generations in the woods, cut off from Ireland

and Scotland to the back of us and not yet come up against any established authority over here that was big enough and mean enough to whip us into line.

That's why the old Baptists and Methodists and Presbyterians deserve a lot more credit than they get. The old hell-fire preachers were the only authority between the barbarians and outright anarchy. I can see them in my mind holding their pulpits like knife-fighters, backed up against the wall clawing and fighting for the Lord. They preached salvation plus the Ten Commandments, and they beat the message into the hard heads of those wild Ulstermen. After a while, men and women who had never seen a sheriff could recite every Thou Shalt Not in the Bible.

Mitch, there's another thing that needs to be said about the old Baptists. The modern man does not give them enough credit for their theology. A lot of churches nowadays have been overrun by greed and fakery, and people have forgotten the old Baptist idea of sin. The old preachers believed that people were born with certain spiritual disabilities and were not likely to overcome them on their own. That belief must not have seemed unreasonable to people who were used to being scuffed around and had to fight to get through every day. They knew they were sorry and sinful and they figured that God, if He had any judgment, held them in pretty low esteem even while He sorrowed for them. They also suspected that mankind was not the most enlightened force in the world. And they did not doubt that there were problems and mysteries out there that were too much for the likes of them.

A lot of the Baptists have outgrown that way of thinking, Mitch. It might surprise you to know that we now have a certain kind of Baptist who thinks that God spends all day worrying about him, personally. He bows his head before he leaves for work (Baptists don't get on their knees to pray any more) and he says, "God, I need to sell $200,000 worth of life insurance today to meet my quota. And it's not just a matter of meeting my quota, God; I've got a payment due on the motorboat, and if I don't sell that insurance I'll be late with the payment. So, God, I want you to go with me today and help me to do what has to be done. I know you'll be there with me, God. Thy rod and Thy staff, they comfort me!"

I guess the modern Baptist is the wave of the future. You may fret a little, from the grave, over what people choose to call success nowadays. But you won't find much fretting among your own descendants. Their idea of success is to have two houses, one that is stationary, with three indoor toilets, and another one that is built on wheels so they can visit Texas without having to pack a suitcase.

I have a little business from time to time at the Washington County Sale Barn, where they auction hogs and cattle. I always feel a little tacky. I drive to town in a pickup truck that is six years too old, and I walk into the auction barn in boots that are $75 too cheap. My hat brim is three inches too narrow. Some of those hillbillies deal in registered cattle, and they haul the steers to the sale barn in factory-built trailers that cost more than my family car. You died too soon, Mitch. You could have been a rancher instead of a farmer if you had held on a few more years.

The modern hillbilly is a man of the world, and he owes it all to one thing, as he sees it: The Lord is on his side. God has chosen the hillbilly for greatness, or at least for prosperity.

Yes, Mitch, the hillbilly and his church have both been modernized. You have to go to the end of the road now, to some place like Aly Baptist Church, to find the old ideas like Original Sin.

I know a Baptist preacher named Will Campbell. He lives at the end of a road in Tennessee. He got into a quarrel with a modern thinker one time. The other fellow was pushing the notion that all men are good and decent, if you look deep enough inside of them. Preacher Campbell said that was not right. "All men are bastards," he said, "and God loves them, anyway."

That's what all the old Baptists preached, as you well remember. They believed that people were born in sin and not likely to improve without outside help. They also believed that the world was a rotten place and not apt to get any better. I guess William Faulkner was a sort of Baptist. He kept telling us that the best we could hope to do, considering the condition of the world, was to bear up and hang on.

Well, Mitch, a lot of the modern church people have gone on ahead of that way of thinking. They don't worry about sin any more. They've got technology, and if you have the right technology you can get around any kind of a problem.

I know a Baptist church in Atlanta, Georgia, that has 5,000 members. They've got a computer to keep up with all of them, and do the bookkeeping, besides. They don't sing "The Old Rugged Cross." A fellow plays Tchaikovsky for them on a pipe organ. You will get an argument out of these folks if you try to tell them that the world is not getting better and better every day in every way. They believe that progress is a God-given right, like freedom of speech, and that nothing is going to slow us down as long as we pay our tithe and go to prayer meeting. They give lip service to the old theory that Adam made a mistake. But as for the modern Baptist himself being a sinful creature—well, that must refer to someone else. Look how God has blessed me in my business. And with His help, I'll have an even better year next year. The gloomy old notion that man is born in sin, thanks to Adam, and might come up against some things that he can't handle—well, we don't have to worry about that now. We can solve most any problem if we put our minds to it. Maybe God ought to turn His attention to the Chinese, or the Iranians. We don't really need Him any more. Not if we have to feel guilty for owning three cars and a boat, and if He keeps reminding us that Adam was no-account and that we're not much better.

Mitch, there's something else that you would have

trouble understanding if you came back for a visit. When you died, in 1927, the idea of electing a Southerner as President of the United States was so far-fetched that no one even talked about it. Well, hold on to your hat. A fellow from Georgia got elected President in 1976. And guess what happened. The first people to turn against him after he got in office were the Southerners.

I don't know, Mitch. I can't explain it. The only thing I can figure is that this fellow was too old-fashioned a Christian. He kept preaching that we had to take care of the poor people and the people who were being run over. So the Southerners, these up-to-date Baptists, turned him out. You see, Mitch, the new Christianity does not have much room for bleeding hearts. Your modern Christian is too smart for that kind of thing. He knows that in today's world, it's every man for himself, and his job is to elbow his way up to God's ear before the next fellow does.

Well, Mitch, I didn't mean to get off on theology, but I wanted to give you a report on the Baptists. I know that you were considered by some to be a good man, and one reason was the Baptist Church. It kept you in line. It kept you reminded of who you were. Some of us nowadays would rather not know who we are. We like to think that we outgrew the old Baptists about the time we outgrew being Arkansawyers. The hillbillies have not had much humility since they became Arkansans.

Some hillbillies will not own up to being Arkansans any more. They have advanced so far that they consider themselves Americans. Look what happened to the community of Aly. Your descendants alone would have tripled the population if they had stayed there. But they have scattered in all directions, and Aly has nearly disappeared. I say all directions, but that is not quite right. The hillbilly considers it effete to migrate east. You've got grandchildren by the dozens in Texas and California, but very few east of the Mississippi.

Mitch, here's something you'll get a kick out of. The

125

Reed family has become so respectable that it has rehabili-
tated its reputation. Nobody talks any more about your
quarreling and fighting with that old Confederate veteran.
Nobody ever mentions that relative of ours who turned
into a bootlegger and knocked up the neighbor girl. I don't
want to be too tough on him, though. I guess that Ulster
blood is hard to get rid of. After a family has lived for a
hundred years in the plain damned wilderness, and spent
no telling how many generations before that fighting the
Catholics and sweating for the gentry, and before that fighting the clans and sweating for the lairds, and then discovering that the sons of bitches preferred sheep on their land
instead of people—after all that, I guess it's not surprising
that a wayward gene crops up now and then and gets us
into trouble.

It's easy to understand why a man with a history like
yours would settle in a place like Yell County, where, on
most days, he could mind his own business. It must puzzle
you that your people left Aly after all the trouble you went
to in settling there. They started leaving before you died, as
you remember. During the 1920s, the young ones started
looking for a way out as soon as they learned to drive a
Model T Ford.

I think it is a fair guess that the people at Aly never
knew anything about progress until they built the bridge
over Irons Creek. You remember that. They had to build the
bridge to accommodate the Model T. Mules and horses
could pull a wagon right across the creek bed, but an automobile might get its magneto wet, or some other private
part, so they had to build bridges. As soon as they got the
bridges built, Grandpa Reed and Mr. Swaim and the others
figured out that they could go to Danville and Mount Ida
any time they wanted to, or even Hot Springs. Now and
then somebody would go all the way to Fort Smith, and
come back and talk about it. I reckon that's how progress
came to Yell County. Henry Ford brought it.

You remember what happened to my daddy, Mitch. He

126

worked around the farm until he was grown. Then he married one of the Meredith girls from Garland County and was never again able to sit still and be a farmer. She got it in her head that they should move to town, because she had seen the Sears and Roebuck catalogue, and all their friends were leaving the hills and hollers. Going to find a better life. Going to town, where water came from a pipe and the toilet was indoors and somebody else killed and cut up the hogs. And the women wore manufactured dresses. And the men wore their hearts out.

Mitch, you may remember the Loyds down at Buckville. After you died, Velma Loyd married a fellow from Indiana named Abbott, and they had a daughter named Shirley. Shirley Abbott has moved to New York and has written a book. It's called *Womenfolks*, and it's about Southern women. Not those flowerdy, sweet-talking beauties from the low country, but the kind that would be called rednecks if they were men. Shirley Abbott is about half kin to us, and I'm acquainted with some of the women in her book. When she says that these women had it rough, she knows what she's talking about. You know it's true. You know how hard the women worked in your day, and how old they looked when they were forty years old. You would say that the men had it rough, too. While the women were having babies, boiling clothes in a black pot, cooking in the yard, sewing clothes, and digging in the garden, the men were clearing the woods with an axe, breaking the horses with raw nerve, building barns and houses with their bare hands, and plowing the fields from daylight until dark.

Some women nowadays, mainly city women, like to say that country men like you did not work very hard, that you slept half the morning, then lit your pipe and ordered the women around until you felt like calling the dogs and going to the woods to hunt. There probably were men like that, but I never heard of any in our family or in the families that our people were friendly with. The country men that I knew had callouses on their hands and arthritis in their joints. Some of them had one eye or a crooked arm because the axe slipped or the horse ran away with the cultivator.

Anyway, the men and women both were glad to get out when they got the chance. They moved to town and the men took up barbering and selling insurance, and the women got washing machines. Nearly all of them are prospering now, as I said before. And they are the unhappiest people I know.

I am speaking mainly of the first generation that left the country. My daddy's generation. About all that is left of them is a band of widows. They spend their days in shopping malls looking for do-dads and having their hair fixed.

These bitter old widows come from a long line of tough women and they are puzzled by their wretchedness. They talk sometimes about the women who stayed behind, and now and then one will admit that she envies the country sisters. The country women seem to be happier. The widows cannot understand that, because it flies in the face of the great dream.

From where I sit writing this letter, I can see down the valley of Hogeye Creek. A young mother of my acquaintance is cleaning a chicken house this morning down in the valley. She and her husband raise chickens for a big poultry company. This is a kind of sharecropping, Mitch. The farmer does the work and takes the risk, and the company takes the profit. A chicken house with 20,000 fryers cooped up inside puts off a powerful smell. A city person will wander into one now and then and the smell will knock him to his knees. The country people are used to it. My young friend working down there today probably has not given it a thought. She is a country woman, and the odor of manure is not considered strange in the country. She might gag on the chemical smell of an office copying machine, but a chicken house does not bother her. Those old widows who left the country fifty years ago have forgotten what manure smells like. They have forgotten how to wring a

128

chicken's neck. They have forgotten what warm blood feels like on the butcher block. They don't have to be tough any more, and they know in some vague way that they have lost something.

I know, Mitch; I don't have to be tough, either. No, I don't want to go back to outdoor toilets and plowing the rocks twelve hours a day. And no, I don't want my wife to wash clothes on a rub-board with lye soap. I do find it strange, though, that we lost that whole generation of men. Why do you suppose a man like my daddy could survive bucking steers, killer horses and copperhead snakes but could not stay alive in the city? None of them could. All the men died too young when they moved to town. I guess they wore themselves out on the pavement, running after the dream.

Mitch, you would have thought that some pied piper was going up and down the country roads, calling the young men and women out of the corn rows and filling their heads with visions.

Dad knew that he had made a mistake. He worked in every grocery and hardware store in South Hot Springs. He would stay at a place until some store on up Hobson Avenue offered him a dollar a week more, and he would switch. By 1936, he was working 10 hours a day selling furniture and earning $15 a week.

One day he heard that a farm was for rent at Buckville. It was a farm that he knew, tucked into a bend of the Ouachita River forty miles from Hot Springs. Not more than thirty acres, but all of it rich bottomland. He had to have it. Not buy it, Mitch; you know that he couldn't have raised the money to buy thirty acres of river bottom land. But it could be had for a reasonable rent, and he had to try. He had to get back to the country. Even then, as young as he was, he knew that he could not stay alive on paved streets.

He packed up the family in a secondhand Model A Ford and moved us back to the farm. He enjoyed living there. Not that he made any money; nobody made any money in Buckville. We all suspected that Mr. Bradley, who owned the store, had a few dollars, and everybody knew that old Mr. Beard had buried a lot of gold in the woods. But other than that, no one had any money in Buckville. I think their expectations did not include money. They had plenty of food and the kids had shoes, at least in the winter. I don't know where the idea came from that the hillbillies nearly starved during the Depression. Maybe people starved in the Delta, where the planters were in charge, but I never heard of many people going hungry in the hills—not around Buckville, anyway. There was one winter a few years earlier that I have heard my mother speak of. Dad had taken the family to Colorado for a year and had come home broke to Yell County. There was no food, except a little meal with weevils in it. An uncle lent us a cow. Mother says the milk kept me alive.

I heard Sam Rayburn's biographer on the radio the other day. He said that when Sam was growing up, the Rayburn family had only forty acres of cotton land near Bonham, Texas, and that they had "barely survived." How do you like that, Mitch? "Barely surviving" with forty acres of good land! We had considerably less land than that at Buckville, but when we left the farm for good it was not necessity that drove us off. We lasted two years, and did not go to bed hungry a single night. We left because we had been corrupted. The country had not changed, but we had. We had tasted soda pop. We had experienced the fine addicting pleasure of running water and flush toilets. Most of all, I think, my mother had discovered the gambler's thrill of living among people with ambitions.

She had already begun to train me to be a gentleman, and to speak a second language so that I could go into the world and be understood. Mitch, I think that's one reason we lost my daddy's generation of men. They had to strain themselves every day to speak a strange tongue. My generation has got used to it, like the smell of a chicken house. You can still hear the old country language now and then of

130

an evening when two or three are gathered together over whiskey. But in the daytime, nearly everybody speaks American now.

That brings you up to date on the family, except for me. I'm not sure how to describe my own condition. I'm still a hillbilly, but I have grown careless about remembering it. I was sorted out and sent away, like an apple that the machine rejects for being the wrong shape or the wrong size. I've been places and done things that don't set well with the family. I'm back home now, but I still can't pass through the sorting machine. That doesn't matter to anyone but me, and the only time it bothers me is when I think about dying. I don't have a place to be buried.

Other than that, I guess, I can't complain. I was reading the Winslow column in the *Washington County Observer* the other day, and down among the births and strokes and family visits, I came across an item that read, in its entirety, as follows: "Velt Shepherd is holding his own." I do not know Velt, but I think I can say that I'm doing about as well as he is.

Well, Mitch, I have put it off as long as I can. That piece of news I mentioned in the beginning is not going to make you rest any more peacefully, but a Union veteran who chose to stay in Arkansas does not have room to criticize somebody else for flouting history. Here it is, Mitch: John Pendleton Reed, my son, your great-great-grandson, is getting ready to marry a Catholic. Not just a Catholic, but an *Ulster* Catholic: one of the original enemy. Born and raised in County Antrim not a hundred miles from where our king whipped the socks off of theirs; brought up in bloody Belfast where our kind has fought her kind every twenty years for four hundred years; where the slogans on the walls, fresh-painted, still say "Kill the Prods" on her side of town and on our side "Remember 1690—Never Surrender!" Marrying an Ulster Catholic, after ten generations in the wilderness hating her, sight unseen.

This is the first time, Mitch, that our family has com-

131

mitted this particular breach. I suppose that's what makes it news. As for why the two of them are doing it, that's hard to explain. This is just a guess, but I think that what has happened is a kind of oversight. Some of the new generation have forgotten to hate. A lapse, you might say—like my failure to vote Republican after three generations of following Mr. Lincoln. A forgetfulness like this comes upon a family now and again. Some old treasure, or grievance, just slips away.

I don't know how her family feel about it. I think ours will be a little disgruntled. They are not too torn up about the threat from Rome any more, but they will not like losing the old hatred. They will miss it.

There is loss all around us, though. Ever since you left, the family treasures and burdens have been slipping away. I suppose that we can stand to lose one more.